Joy Songs,
Trumpet Blasts,
And
Hallelujah Shouts!

Sermons
In The African-American
Preaching Tradition

Carlyle Fielding Stewart, III

CSS Publishing Company, Inc., Lima, Ohio

Some scripture quotations are from the *New Revised Standard Version of the Bible*, copyright © 1989 by the Division of Christian Education of the National Council of Churches of Christ in the USA. Used by permission.

Some scripture quotations are from the *Holy Bible, New International Version.* Copyright © 1973, 1978, 1984 International Bible Society. Used by permission of Zondervan Bible Publishers. All rights reserved.

Some scripture quotations are from the *Amplified New Testament,* copyright © 1954, 1958, 1987, by The Lockman Foundation. Used by permission.

Some scripture quotations are from the *King James Version of Bible*, in the public domain.

Library of Congress Cataloging-in-Publication Data

Stewart, Carlyle Fielding, 1951-
  Joy songs, trumpet blasts, and hallelujah shouts : twelve sermons in the African-American preaching tradition / Carlyle Fielding Stewart, III
      p.   cm.
  Includes bibliographical references.
  ISBN 0-7880-0855-2
  1. Sermons, American—Afro-American authors. 2. Afro-American preaching. I. Title.
BV4241.5.S84   1997
252'.0089'96073—dc20
                                                          96-38671
                                                              CIP

ISBN: 0-7880-0855-2   PRINTED IN U.S.A.

For

The Rev. Dr. Joseph Roberts, Jr.

and

The Rev. Dr. Charles Gilchrist Adams

Two Great Preachers of Our Times!

Table of Contents

Introduction

Ever since slave preachers whirled, moaned, and chanted their camp fire audiences into ethereal ecstasy, the gifts of black preaching have been a hallmark of the American cultural experience. That black preaching has always contained a unique style of content and delivery cannot be disputed, for, as Henry Mitchell has observed, the development of a black hermeneutic in preaching has been a major tool of survival for African-American people. "How shall they hear without a preacher?" might be paraphrased to, "How could black people have survived without the gifts and genius of black preaching?"

Preaching, "saying it," or "bringing the Word from on high" has always been a important rite in the African-American experience. The oral and narrative remnants of African culture have been retained in the American context and are perpetuated in the fervent desire of black people to tell the story and hear the Word. The ritual drama and processes, the form and substance of the art of storytelling to black audiences is an important dimension of African-American life and a chief element in the preservation of black people's sanity and a principal catalyst in their quest for human freedom and dignity.

In a repressively hostile and racist society, where oral traditions were carefully monitored by slave masters and brutal overlords, the spoken word had cosmic reverberations and thus took on ethereal, magical significance for both story hearer and story teller. "Telling it" created and sustained its own cultural archives and liturgies for human survival. Telling it like it really is through self-created cultural idioms and nuances shaped the order, ethos, and chaos of African-American existence and laid the groundwork for black preaching as a unique art form.

Thus the role of the black preacher in interpreting and translating the adversities of the American experience into a viable transcendent, psycho-spirituality and litany of social protest cannot be underestimated, for words have their own vitality, shape their own consciousness, and create their own context for interpreting and constructing social and spiritual reality. The Word of God moving across the lips of the messenger contained even greater power in not only shaping consciousness and belief in the hearers but also in "transporting" them to other worlds and realms. If the black slave was limited geographically to a specific place, the Word of God issuing from the black preacher carried him into other spaces and places where only he and not his master had the privilege of going.

Thus the success of black preaching cannot be solely determined, like its Anglo-American counterpart, by conventional hermeneutics and the typical taxonomies of sermonic development, but by how closely akin its dynamics and forms approximate the structures of consciousness and orbicular ethos of African-American culture.[1]

In other words, black preaching is more than simple oratory or verbalization, but a form of spiritual alchemy, of conjuring and medicinizing, of incantational litanizing, which affects not only the spiritual transfiguration of believers but the transformation of the created order of society and the universe. Words are not mere words in the lexicon of vocabularies of cultures, but pharmacies dispensing their own cures, infirmaries creating their own vehicles and vernaculars for healing, respite, and spiritual and social transformation. The spoken Word of God contains the power not only to re-churn the soulscape of believers, but also to re-seed the landscape of society, thus resulting in the new creation.

This book does not classify black preaching according to traditional categories of interpretation. Henry Mitchell, J. Alfred Smith, Evans Crawford, and others have done outstanding work in facilitating a deeper knowledge of the why, how, and what of black preaching as an art form. James Earl Massey has also done significant work on sermon design and structure.[2]

This work cites the uniqueness of black preaching from a different angle. Rather than employ such categories as **expository,** **topical,** and **narrative** as a means for placing and categorizing the following sermons, I use such terms as "poetic," "imaginative," "medicinal," or "transformational" as ways of describing both the form and intent of the sermon. While these sermons might well be categorized as expository, narrative or topical in the traditional, structural sense, I believe that black preaching ultimately embraces but exceeds these classifications. J. Alfred Smith in his work *Preach On* also develops other categories depicting the nature of black preaching.

Thus we forgo the traditional modes of interpretation because the forms and rhythms, the colors and nuances which touch the souls of black believers and shape consciousness are the principal elements of black sermonizing. Categorization according to the traditional formulas, while cognitively helpful in historically placing black sermons within the sacred traditions of Christian preaching, does not capture the soul essence or distinctive elements of black preaching as a *sui generis* art form. Any attempt to codify or catalogue black preaching in any peremptory or exhaustive sense however is certainly impossible. But to adopt other nomenclatures to describe this unique art form is especially helpful in casting a different light on the gifts of black preaching.

In order to unearth the deeper elements of black preaching, it is necessary to view it through different lenses. Having said this, let us turn our attention to these various forms of black preaching by describing their different characteristics.

---

1. We often analyze preaching according to the structures of thought and sermonic construction. A more important idea is fathoming the ways black sermonizing speaks to the structures of consciousness inherent in black life and culture. So the critical idea here is not simply how the sermon is structured *ipso facto* but how closely it relates to the structures of thought and the patterns of analysis and the culture of consciousness in African-American life.

2. See Henry Mitchell's *Black Preaching*, (Nashville: Abingdon Press, 1990); *Preaching For Black Self-esteem*, (Nashville: Abingdon Press, 1994); J. Alfred Smith's *Preach On*, (Nashville: Broadman Press, 1984); James Earl Massey, *Designing The Sermon*, (Nashville: Abingdon Press, 1980, ed. William Thompson). See also, Evan Crawford and Thomas H. Troegers' *The Hum: Call and Response in African-American Preaching*, (Nashville: Abingdon Press, 1995); James Forbes' *The Holy Spirit and Preaching*, (Nashville: Abingdon Press, 1989); and H. Beecher Hicks' *Preaching Through a Storm*, (Grand Rapids: Zondervan, 1987).

Black Preaching:
A Four-Cornered Universe

The four elements of black preaching might also be called the four corners of the art. As stated earlier, our aim is to shed light on the uniqueness of black preaching as a celebrated art form. While traditional categories are helpful in grasping the structure of black sermons and their functional value, the way sermons move and empower black audiences and reach their desired objectives is more important. Thus the description of black preaching as a four-cornered universe is designed to identify the functional nature of black sermons. While narrative, expository, and other forms of sermonizing also have specific functions accompanying their structures, we employ different descriptions which reflect more precisely the dynamics of the African-American oral traditions.

Thus we say that black preaching has four primary functions or descriptions which distinguish it from other forms of sermonizing. The four tiers of black preaching are **poetic recitation, imaginative insight, spiritual pharmacology,** and **spiritual and social transformation.**

I. Black Preaching as Poetic Recitation

To appreciate black preaching as a unique art form, we must grasp its poetic affinities. We cannot fathom the deeper currents of black sermonizing from a strictly prose viewpoint. While the sermon in written form is prose in the conventional sense of the word, black preaching has closer cognates with the idioms and nuances of poetry.

There is a poetry, a rhythm, a swing to black life and culture which unmistakably differentiates it from the "lived genres" of other peoples and cultures. This poetry can be seen in everything from the walk and talk of African-Americans to the dynamics and forms of African-American culture. Black preaching which is successful in reaching the black masses closely reflects the rhythms and poetic inflections of African-American life. This does not mean that sermonizing in other traditions and cultures does not bear marks of the poetic. It only means that the poetic aspects of black preaching are closely aligned with the poetry of black life in general. Such poetry creates its own metaphors and litanies for human existence and shapes specific idioms and expectations about communication among black people.

As a "poetry people," the oral nature of our cultural traditions has helped us cultivate our own hermeneutics of rhythm, create our own world orientation and ethos, and preserve litanies of existence as fluid as the Nile River. Our cognitive-spiritual orientation is primarily poetic, wherein the rhythms of the universe and life itself create their own harmonic and melodic structures of human interpretation which both undergird and inform our perception and action in the world around us.

While our being in the world and style of existence is principally poetic, our ways of knowing and grasping, of feeling and thinking contain an aesthetic value essential to our cognitive and spiritual well-being. Thus every aspect of our lives is poetry. Our sanity and freedom as a people are intimately bound to our capacity to diversify the verse of our jangled existence; to transform our discord into some resonant, sonorous life-giving, life-fulfilling possibility. This is the poetic genre of black life in America. It is a lived experience which creates its own values and linguistic structures of black existence.

Such poetry is manifested from our cognitive structure patterns to the melodic way we turn our phrases, for there is an incessant beat to our striving, a rhythmic pulsation, a fluidity of movement, a penchant to elevate our spirituality to higher levels of self-realization. The poetic inclination of black preaching captures the essence of black life and culture in America as does no other medium. For black people, then, the rhythms and dynamics of how things are said are just as significant as the content of what is said. Part of our cognitive and spiritual proclivity accentuates the poetry of rhythm as well as the prose of form. We think, act, and have our being rhythmically. The rhythms of black culture create their own structures of consciousness which inform the way we grasp and express the fundamental truths of black life.

What the black preacher says may well speak to my mind, but the real question is: Does it speak to my soul? Is it emotive? Is it cognitive and rhythmic? Does it take me to higher realms of conscious reality? Black preaching as poetry reaches the soul of believers in ways that black preaching as prose cannot. This does not mean that manuscript preaching in prose form cannot be poetic. But there is something about the poetry of black preaching that reaches into corridors of being where prose dares not go. The rhythms and fires of the poetic venue in black sermonizing both escalate and titillate the spiritual sensibilities of black believers. It reaches black audiences in ways which distinguish it from other forms of sermonizing.

When we say that black preaching is poetic, we are suggesting that it not only provides a mode of cognitive-spiritual orientation which reaches black hearers, but a manner of delivery, a type of content and structure which contain various forms of alliteration, narrative storyizing, and imagination which distinguish it from all other forms of preaching. The subtleties, phrasings, inflections, nuances, and imaginative reachings of speech reminiscent of all great poetry is a hallmark of black preaching. The preacher might use a manuscript or preach extemporaneously, but the poetic metaphor creates the context from which the sermon emerges. Whether stringing together rhymes of comedic verse or metaphorically painting "still shots" or "landscapes" with swift-quick strokes of the verbal brush, the black preacher is a poet of sorts, whose artistic leanings and longings are his passports into the minds and hearts of hearers.

Listen to black preaching steeped in the rich folk traditions of African-American culture and there you will discover a rhythm, a tone that sets its own order, creates its own liturgy, conjures its own litany, and colors its own world with peculiar nuances while still ordering the chaos of human experience. The rhythm and poetry of black preaching can be found in the cadences of the sea, in the metered vacillation of night and day, in the measured mutation of all things living. Whether the hoop, the moan, the elongated groan, or the telephonic resonation of a rhythmic incantation, it is poetry, pure poetry, seeing and hearing the black preacher take the wings of the morning.

Those who value preaching as only prose find it difficult to grasp the deeper poetic shadings and significations of black preaching as a celebrated art form. The syncopations endemic to oral culture are different than those of predominantly literary culture. As one white friend and colleague once commented, "If I could just get into the rhythm of what he was saying, I could have followed the sermon through. I just got lost in his rhythm."

The difference was that my friend was used to preaching that carried him by foot rather than preaching that transported him by horseback. A rhythmic difference exists between the ride and the walk. The modes of transportation and rhythms of journeying are wholly different. The problem was the sermon "walks" to which he was accustomed weren't even brisk walks at that, but slow, disjointed wanderings devoid of purpose or cohesion. Unaccustomed to traveling by horse, he was thrown from his "saddle" five minutes into the sermon, although the preacher began with a slow "gallop."

A further encumbrance was his predominantly prose orientation to reality. A poetic orientation would have made him more receptive to the rhythms of recitation which are hallmarks of black sermonizing.

Great poetry and great black preaching are not only rhythmic but visionary. They have elements of timing and versification essential to the reader's and hearer's sense of sound and sight, place and time. Poetry and preaching entreat sensory and cognitive participation in ways unmatched by other genres and idioms. The poet invites the reader to enter into his or her vision of reality. Black preaching as poetic recitation compels hearers to sense both viscerally and cerebrally the world of the Gospel, to enter into and scale higher heights spiritually, to catch sight of the preacher's beatific or cataclysmic vision of the reality of God as revealed in scripture. From the way the preacher begins his sermon to his orgasmic ascent towards the spiritual climax is all poetic adventure, an introit to the high tides of spiritual exploration. Those who would enter into these spiraling crescendos of ethereal elevation must fathom the poetic demeanor of black preaching to appreciate fully both the design and intent of black sermonizing as a true art form.

Black preaching as poetic recitation is one story in the four-cornered universe of black sermonizing. The vision, rhythms and forms of versification contained in the art of poetry are properties of great black preaching. This is a very important aspect in understanding one function of black preaching in its four-storied universe.

II. Black Preaching as Imaginative Insight

Traditional hermeneutics often underscore the importance of acquiring biblical tools in analyzing and deciphering the true meaning of biblical texts. Biblical exegesis is a process by which the preacher determines the true intent of a particular passage of scripture by employing specific criteria for evaluation, such as the writer of the text, time, intent and purpose of writing, audience and other important elements which will help disclose the true "design" of the author. Invariably, in determining the form and pericope of any text, the preacher must devote time to analyzing both the text and the context of scripture. Such analyses are often influenced by what the text literally and figuratively says rather than what it does not say.

A hallmark of black preaching has been its ability to imaginatively take the things not said in the text and apply them to today's context in ways which provide new insight and meaning into the biblical text and black hearers. While traditionalists may view this as a form of isogesis or interpolation because it does not follow the conventional formulas of exegesis, it nevertheless is a legitimate hermeneutic according to Henry Mitchell and others.

Important here for black audiences is that text is related to their specific context; that the Gospel make sense according to the ethos of the African-American experience. One can exegete thoroughly, and this should be highly encouraged, but the end result must be that black hearers must make sense of the text in light of their own experience. A correlation must therefore exist between what occurs in the text and what transpires in the context of believers who hear the message.

My contention is that while historically black preachers as a rule may not have always meticulously followed the rules of exegesis in discerning a text, there always has been a hermeneutics of imagination which correlates the biblical text and experiential context of hearers in ways which do not violate the integrity of scripture. In other words, extant in black preaching is a cultural hermeneutic or a biblical dynamic always closely approximating the mood, ambiance, and aesthetics of scriptural passages while coalescing them with the cultural ethos and linguistic propensities of black audiences. These portraits of the text are disseminated in the idioms which are very close to both biblical and contemporary milieu.

While the structural norms of exegesis may not always be followed closely, black sermonizing emotively and aesthetically is not far from the mood and milieu of specific texts. In this case, we have a hermeneutics of imagination or aesthetic which allows the preacher to search those spoken and unspoken aspects of the text in an attempt not only to help hearers make sense of the text but also to reveal how it intersects with their lives presently. If critics say the essential idea of the text is not captured because of the lack of structural exegesis, the essential mood or backdrop of the text which informs the extant or secondary truths of the texts themselves may be disclosed in ways that still help hearers grasp the fundamental truths and milieu of the scriptural passage.[1]

In other words, is there some other way that I might grasp the central ideas, moods, colors, nuances or truths of the text without fundamentally following the rules of exegesis? To answer this question is to delve into the deeper realities of the success of black preaching as imaginative insight. While the black preacher may not have traditionally followed all the rules of exegesis, it does not thwart the revelation of some fundamental truth of either the text of scripture or the context of the hearer, that is, the written text or the experiential context, which creates, resonates, and informs its own truth in ways which do not violate the integrity and trajectory of the biblical record.

The imaginative insight of black preaching has truly been one of its great gifts, for to tell the story and capture the ethos of the biblical background in ways that make sense to black hearers has been one of the outstanding contributions of black preaching as an art form. This imaginative insight has been most maligned, negated, and even dismissed. It is invariably assailed by those whose structural orientation cannot appreciate the unique aspects of black preaching or those who do not value the unique folk traditions of

African-American culture which evolved from the survival traditions of African-American people.

This imaginative insight contains a whole welter of media which are essential to facilitating an understanding of the text. The creative imagination of black preachers has done much to bring texts to life in ways reminiscent of no other preaching. Imaginative insight can be seen in everything from the cultivation of catchy sermon titles to the peculiar narrative styles adopted to illuminate the central ideas of a text. Drama, allegory, metaphor, simile, and other idioms are not incongruous to black sermonizing.

Historically speaking, the use of imaginative insight was particularly useful for slave preachers who were unable to read and had to rely on their creative imagination to develop sermons that fired and inspired their audiences.

Black culture has always been the primary archive of black preaching and the seedbed of black creativity and thought. One must therefore grasp and appreciate its peculiarities to fathom the deeper realities of black preaching as a cognitive and imaginative enterprise.

I stated earlier that this imaginative insight was expressed in what the preacher interpreted about the unsaid portions of the text. For example, I recall hearing a sermon about what the prodigal son experienced that was not revealed in the Gospel record. The preacher developed his sermon around the experience of being a down-and-outer. The sermon was titled, "Every Good-bye Ain't Gone." Only those familiar with the ethos of the black cultural experience could understand where the preacher was coming from in this sermon. The preacher used imagination to develop his title and sermon about the unspoken portions of the text. He dramatized the feelings of being truly prodigal and described in detail such sentiments. The sermon's success lay in its capacity to help hearers see those unwritten aspects of the text through imagination. Questions were consistently raised in relation to those unsaid dimensions of the text. What was it like to live in a pigsty? What feelings of loneliness and rejection did the son feel and how do we relate this text to our own feelings of being lonely in today's world?

The creative development of ideas through imaginative insight is essential in an age where preaching is in "competition" with so many other media. The preacher must be creative without being pedantic, insightful without being boring. Because preaching competes with so many other idioms in present society, the preacher must be in touch with the creative elements of his art. In a video culture where hearing is conditioned by seeing, where camera angles in films are sustained no longer than six seconds per frame, people become easily bored with preaching that is not precocious, creative, dynamic, and dramatic. People are accustomed to movement which is largely conditioned by the dramatic idioms of our media culture. They want to see movement and feel that the sermon is taking them somewhere they haven't been.

Countless other examples can be cited of black preachers creatively developing sermons in ways that make good sense to black hearers. I cannot possibly delineate them all here, but the fact is imaginative insight is another aspect which differentiates black preaching from other forms of sermonizing.

III. Black Preaching as Spiritual Pharmacology

I stated earlier that black preaching is a form of alchemy: a means of healing the hearers of their pain and hurts. This might sound strange to some, but the truth is the black preacher is a shaman of sorts, a cosmic conjurer, a medicine medium who provides regular doses of a prescriptive cure for the congregation's ailments. The medicinal aspects of black preaching as an art form can be observed in what is said and how it is said.

The "whoop" so characteristic of black preaching may well have begun as a ritual ceremony to petition the healing and magical powers of the Holy Ghost. (A close affinity exists between the Buddhist and African ceremonial chants and the whoop of black preaching.) Black preaching is not only an invocation of the healing presence of God, but a ritual confirmation of the Spirit's power to uplift, heal, and redeem black lives.

Black preaching historically has had medicinal value for multitudes of African-Americans. When black people could not have access to the conventional forms of healing, except homeopathic remedies, medicinal intervention also occurred through oral communication and the idiom of preaching. The preacher's ability to call down the Holy Ghost and inspire hearers to envision God's revelation through the spoken Word was a remarkable element of black preaching which is often taken for granted today. The black preacher has been and still is a kind of medicine man who speaks "cures" to the ills of hearers through spiritual pharmacology.

The power of medicine men and women in traditional African society lay precisely in their capacity to speak into reality those therapies, conjurations, and personal transformations which enable believers to be healed of their spiritual and physical pain. The African-American preacher has had a similar role in healing the pain, sorrow, and suffering of black people in America. For the uttered Word possesses the power to effect spiritual, physical, and social transformation, and this dynamic aspect of black preaching distinguishes it from other forms of sermonizing.

Thus a central function of black preaching has been its medicinal value. The gift of black sermonizing is not the mere utterance of words, couched poetically within the sacred idioms of African-American culture, but its capacity to effect positive spiritual change by successfully imploring the power and presence of the Holy Ghost for the dynamic transformation of black lives.

Black life in America is a soulful experience. Spirituality, personal well-being, and identity are all intimately bound to the reality of the black soul. The way we sing and the way we shout, the way we laugh, think, and experience the fullness of our being resonates with the reality of soul. Great black preaching provides a medicine-cure to black souls struggling for sanity, order, and light amid the turmoil and benightment of their existential circumstances.

Often, in an effort to compare black with white preaching, this medicinal aspect of black sermonizing is sadly overlooked. Blacks have traditionally called this "seeking the fix" from the preacher, much like a patient seeks a cure or prescription from a physician. Black churchgoers not only desire to hear the Word, but want a soul cure, to be "fixed" in a manner that will bring about healing in their lives.

A thorough study should be conducted to analyze these medicinal dimensions in African-American sermonizing. In doing so, one would unequivocally discover similarities between the work of traditional medicine men, shamans, and healers in African traditional societies and African-American preachers.

We can also see this therapeutic function in black worship. For example, the hallelujah shout of black worshippers is not only an acclamation of God's goodness and power, but a kind of therapy; an expression of human freedom; a means of releasing the dross and dread of daily existence. It is an affirmation of God's healing, transforming, and redemptive power in black life. The worship experience itself is not only a practice of human freedom but a ritual drama wherein participants engage in spiritual acts of healing and transcendence through music, prayers, healing, teaching, and preaching.

The "word magic" of black preaching heals lives by telling the story in the idioms and ethos of African-American culture. It also has a corroborative function in that it clarifies and comforts those souls wallowing in the quagmires of personal despair. Words heal, rejuvenate, quicken consciousness, and inspire black audiences to "make it through the week."

The medicinal aspect of black preaching has been and is a key element in the psycho-spiritual healing and liberation of black people. As a parishioner once remarked, "Black preaching helps me to make sense of it all. It helps me to understand that I'm all right and that God will take care of things in the by-and-by."

The healing components of black preaching cannot be negated or obviated, for healing comes in many forms: prayer, laying on of hands, humor, and pure, unadulterated prophetic preaching of the Gospel. The black church and preaching have always been healing reservoirs for African-American people, where the lost are found, the broken made whole, and the confused and beleaguered clarified and nurtured.

When no hospitals and infirmaries would take us in, and no therapists and social workers were available to help us maintain the strength of our sanity, the sermon and the black church became the bulwark of spiritual vitality. No other institution or individual surpasses the black church and the black preacher in reaching, teaching, and healing the souls of the masses of African-American people. This healing dynamic of African-American preaching is still one of the most important dimensions of the black preaching tradition. To find a balm in Gilead to heal the wounded soul is of paramount interest to preaching in the African-American tradition.

IV. Black Preaching as Spiritual and Social Transformation

The upshot of much black preaching is to effect positive transformation of black life in America. This involves both social protest and spiritual transformation. The face of reality, with all its ugliness and pain, must be transfigured into a new awareness of the self and God and their myriad possibilities. Black preaching seeks to create a context for the spiritual transfiguration and social transformation of black existence. The goal is to herald the new heaven and earth, to actively establish the kingdom of God within the individual and the larger society.

Transformation and transfiguration are key words because invariably the intent is to enable hearers to envision themselves as dynamic agents for positive change. Much of black preaching puts hearers in touch with the possibilities and mandates for spiritual and social transformation. God is a God of progress and change and believers must be equipped to implement changes which will establish a more wholesome existence.

Since slavery, one consistent theme pervading the lives of African-Americans has been progress, the discovery and cultivation of those human and material resources which improve the economic and spiritual condition of our people. An underlying theme of much black sermonizing is the need for change and acquiring the courage to change with God's help.

The elements of transfiguration and transformation are not only manifested in how black people proactively change their lives and communities after hearing the sermon, but how they respond to the message while hearing it. The fruits of spiritual transfiguration can be seen in everything from the shout to praise incantations during the worship experience. The worship service becomes a theater of personal transfiguration as parishioners respond to the word in various ways. The realities of spiritual and personal transfiguration are ever present in black worship and are important parts of black preaching and black church life. The reality of freedom experienced in personal transfiguration must also translate into the social realm. Suffice it not to run, shout, praise, and pray; one must translate that spiritual transformation into acts of protest and resistance against the powers and tyrannies of racism, oppression and disenfranchisement.

It therefore suffices not simply to maintain our condition, plight, or the status quo. The objective is to effect positive change, to help people experience the life-transforming, all-enveloping spirit of God which will empower them to stretch beyond the comfort zones of their human circumstances. The preached Word of God is the creative catalyst energizing our quest to transform and be transformed, and this has always been a benchmark of the African-American preaching tradition. Preaching invokes a dramatic change in the lives of God's people and the communities in which they live.

This dimension of black preaching calls to mind the prophetic incentives to spiritual transformation. The black preacher has functioned as both priest and prophet, but invariably the task is to move the people forward in their thinking and to challenge them spiritually at the core of belief in ways which will empower progressive social and spiritual transformation. Transfiguration of both mind and soul are essential to the psycho-spiritual-social liberation of black people in America, and black preaching has always been on the cutting edge of these concerns. The black preacher exhorts so that positive change in black lives will transpire. Black people in hearing black preachers expect that the Word of God will evoke a permanent, if not temporal, transformation of their existence. Spiritual and existential transformation are an integral expectation of both black preachers and their audiences.

We might say further that all of the major radical changes in the corporate life of African-American peoples has been influenced in some form by black preaching and the black church. From slavery to the present moment, the African-American preacher has been a strong influence in the personal and social transformation of African-American people. No other influence has been greater in helping black people face, cope, and surmount the realities of African-American existence.

These four dimensions of black preaching are not exhaustive, but they provide a glimpse into the dynamic elements of the genius of black preaching as an art form. A more lengthy discussion of the culture, power, and freedom of black preaching might be undertaken at a later date.

Suffice that we have provided a brief overview of these four aspects of the African-American preaching tradition. While other traditions might have similar forms and functions in sermonizing, I believe these depictions represent a significant component of African-American sermonizing which has thus far not been thoroughly explicated.

---

1. The notion here is that texts have primary and secondary propositions. The primary ideas are those which are readily disclosed by the text in any cursory reading. The secondary ideas are the deeper psychological, spiritual, or practical truths not readily disclosed in the text itself, which might be captured through imaginative insight. For instance, a primary truth of the story of the prodigal son may be the consequences of disobedience. A secondary insight might be the prodigal son as a personification of the radical aspects of unbridled spirituality. Rather than emphasize the consequences of disobedience and the importance of finding our way home again, we might stress how the prodigal son represents the wild side of our psychological situation. Everyone has a wayward or radical side to one's human personality. This is a secondary idea of the text which is revealed through the use of imagination.

Advent's "Invisible" Man

Matthew 1:18-25

The idea of the invisibility in our culture is no new thing. The great H.G. Wells wrote a book called *The Invisible Man.* In it he imaginatively explores the development of a professor's ingenious use of science to effect his own invisibility. Invisibility becomes a metaphor for invincibility. His becoming invisible is by his own choosing. He literally disappears with the ingestion of a certain chemical solution, which eventually drives him insane. The point here is this man, Griffin, chooses to become whatever he desires, a person who cannot be seen, only heard. Nothingness is the form he ultimately selects as a way of being.

On the other hand, we have the nameless protagonist in that great masterpiece of art by Ralph Ellison. His book *Invisible Man* is a commentary on the invisible status of black people in America. His invisibility, unlike the Wells character, is not by choice, but due to other people's choosing. It is because the larger white culture refuses to acknowledge and recognize the black man as a living entity that he is relegated to the status of non-person or *persona non grata.* Wells' invisible man chooses his fate. Ellison's invisible man has his fate chosen for him by whites who refuse to see his black skin.

Today, in our sermon, there is Advent's "invisible" man. His role of virtual invisibility is not by personal choice like with Wells, nor is it because others have chosen this for him as with Ellison, but because God has called him to occupy such a place in one of the most important events of all time.

The time is Advent. The event is the birth of Jesus. This invisible man's name is Joseph, the father of Jesus. He is not nameless.

He does not, like Griffin in the Wells novel, overdose from his own ambition which leads to his own destruction. He does not struggle to establish his personal identity in a society that has rejected his personhood, like Ellison's nameless protagonist. He has been called by God to be a behind-the-scenes person in this world historical event. He is not center stage. He does not have a leading role. He is not the bandleader or the drum major who saturates the limelight while parading the people of God into a new millennia. He is virtually "invisible" because hardly anyone talks of him. They barely speak his name. He is a mystery, an enigma, a phantasm, an apparition, it seems, which appears for a time, then vanishes from the stage of human history.

Catholics revere Mary, the Holy Mother of God. We know Mary. God chooses and uses her as an instrument of divine intervention. She has high visibility. We know of Elizabeth, and others. We know of shepherds who kept their flocks by night. We know even of the infamous Herod who issued the decree that all baby boys under two years be slaughtered on sight. We know of all the cast and crew of the great pageantry. But Joseph? Who is he? Why in a culture dominated by men is his role so recessed? When the question, "Can any good thing come out of Nazareth?" was asked disbelievingly by others mocking Jesus, could this not have been so much a slur on the town as it was an indirect rebuke of the lineage of Joseph? Who is he anyway? He's too obscure. Too quiet. Too much behind the scenes. Too invisible for our liking.

Advent's "invisible" man is Joseph, father of the baby Jesus. And his invisibility is largely because he is not center stage, but behind the scenes. He is not the leading character but he is in a supportive role to his wife and family.

Yet, despite his seeming invisibility, despite his relatively obscure status, despite the fact that his name is not on the Broadway billboards of the main streets of Jerusalem, he is a man's man because he accepts his role and carries out his responsibility as a man of substance and presence. He is there but not there. He quietly and obediently responds to God's will in his life and leads his family to safety into Egypt under the death threats of Herod.

Yes, he is "invisible," but the imprints of his heroic deeds have made a lasting and indelible imprint on the hearts and souls of all those who have embraced the life of his son Jesus. Yes, he is "invisible," not center stage, not calling the shots, not in control of the strange events which invade his household. He is "invisible," but not completely removed from an important role in Jesus' birth. And this brings us to the first proposition of this sermon:

Advent's invisible man may not have been seen that much but he was a man of substance. We know that he was a man of substance because of the way he responded to God in his dream. He discovered that his fiancee was pregnant with a child, knowing he had not known her, but he still kept her as his very own, married her, and took care of his family.

Joseph was under enormous pressure. In a culture that valued the sanctity of virginity before marriage, he would immediately come under great suspicion by those around him. Many thought that both he and Mary had broken their premarital vows, that they had been as one too soon, and the evidence was immediately forthcoming. She was pregnant with child and the conditions under which Mary received the gift would be highly suspicious. Everyone would know that they had been together.

But a far greater peril was in the mind of Joseph himself. What would he think? How would and could he believe Mary's story about how she was implanted with the baby? There was no in vitro fertilization, no intra-uterine insemination. He would have to rely heavily on her word and on the report he received in his dream from the angels from on high. He could have easily put Mary out. He could have easily written her off, but because he was a man of substance he fulfilled the promises of God.

You don't have to be highly visible to be a man of substance. In today's culture we think of men of substance as those with the brawn and might, those on the gridiron or clay courts who demonstrate their substance through physical prowess. A man of substance in this culture is a Reggie White, a Hulk Hogan, a Charles Barkley, or a physically powerful, well-known man whose name graces billboards. Men of substance are men whose names are household words. Men whose personas fill the silver screens:

matinee idols, dream weavers, the titans of tenacity. Men who lead packs of other men because of their fame and fortune. These are the men of substance in our culture. The men of great visibility. Men who stand up and stand out. Men whose profile is so great they can be seen at 100-yard distances in midnight fog.

But here we have Joseph. He's not kicking behinds and taking names on the gridiron. He's not a member of Herod's imperial guard. He's not a prelate or a priest. Not a prince or a magistrate. Not a gladiator or a Roman terminator. Just a minimum wage worker, trying to take care of his family, trying to keep his baby boy from being murdered by a bloodthirsty, political wanna-be.

You don't have to have a high profile or great visibility to be a man of substance. What made Joseph a man of substance? The fact that he made the right choices amid great odds; that he allowed his conscience to be his guide despite what his friends and family would say about Mary; that he allowed the Spirit of the Lord to lead his humble heart to make a decision which changed eternity. He didn't send her to the clinic for an abortion. He didn't run and hide and cry, "Woe is me." He is a man of substance because he made the decision that a real man would make. He didn't have high visibility in society, but he was a man of great stature in God's eyes because of the decisions he made to be supportive of his fiancee during an anxious time.

There are a lot of high visibility people with no substance at all. I recently heard of a man who got permission from his wife to be present at the delivery of his girlfriend's baby, which turned out to be his son. He's a man of great visibility, but a man of no substance. Rumor is he's looking for a way out of both situations so he can be free of all responsibility.

We need black men today who will stand up and be men; be men enough to nurture the children they've brought into the world. The ledgers of eternity are disgracefully filled with too many deadbeat boys who are would-be men. They're looking for visibility but have no substance. They're looking for glory but have no dash, courage, or resolve to take care of what's theirs!

Joseph was a man of substance because he took on responsibility as God requested. You don't have to have a high profile and

30

great visibility to be a man of substance. Advent's invisible man was a man of substance, despite not being seen that much and not having a leading role in the birth of Jesus.

Second, Advent's invisible man may not have said that much but he was a man of presence. Matthew does not record a single word that Joseph ever utters. He is present. He is at the right place at the right time. He never says a word. Not a single utterance in all of Matthew, but he's always there. You know he's there. You don't hear his words, but you see the imprints of his presence through his deeds. He had to have presence for the angels to reveal themselves to him. His presence had to be opened to the will and power of the Holy Ghost to do what he did.

In this culture we think that presence means talkativeness. Those who are present have to make the most noise to have high visibility. But there are those men who may not say much, but they have presence. They have the confidence to be men. They don't utter many words, but when you need them in the crunch of battle they're there. When all hell breaks loose and the foundations are ripped asunder, they stand tall amid the storms and whirlwinds of life's tragedies and calamities, holding the rails of stability until order is restored. No, they don't say much, but they are truly there.

One man tells the story of when he lost his wife, and he was terribly distraught. His close friend came by. They walked by the seaside and the man poured out his heart to his friend. They walked the bustling streets of New York. His friend never said a word. He just listened and provided a presence that helped the man get through the trial of his life. Presence doesn't always mean words, but caring and being there when people need you most. This is a hallmark of true men.

But there are men who talk a lot and back it up. Thank God for them. They can talk the talk and walk the walk. They too have favor in God's eyes. But it is clear that Joseph's invisibility was heightened by his quiet nature.

Matthew puts no words in Joseph's mouth, but his presence is so vital to the well-being of his family that it is clear they could not have survived without his presence. You don't have to say much, just be much. Have presence and be present when people need you most!

Who waited on Mary hand and foot when she was pregnant with Jesus? Who found the place for them to stay on that cold, windy night when the keepers of the inn turned them away? Who stoked the fires and bailed the hay? Who ran the errands and brought them food to eat? Who kept watch when Herod's lackeys were running wild in the streets looking to smoke the first two-year-old they saw looking anything like a messiah? Who was there at daybreak and midnight? Who buttered the bread and poured the cola? Who turned the straw, counted the sheep, and watered the trough for the animals after the baby was born? Advent's invisible man Joseph, who may not have said much but was present, there in body, mind, and soul, helping eternity to do a new thing in Jesus.

You don't have to talk to be present; just be there. It's not your visibility but your availability that often counts in the things that matter. He never said a mumbling word, but he helped turn Mary's cross into a crown, and he helped give humanity the King of kings, Jesus. He wasn't a captain in the Roman imperial army but he helped preserve the leader of God's salvation army!

Matthew says that after Jesus was born Joseph said something. He gave a name to the child. He didn't say much but he was a man of presence.

Third, Advent's invisible man didn't do that much but he was a man of action. After his first dream about the birth of the child, it says in verse 1:24, he did what the angel of the Lord had commanded him and *took* Mary to be his wife. In Matthew 2:13, the scriptures say that an angel of the Lord appeared to Joseph in a dream and told him to get up and take the child and escape to Egypt. As a man of action he did what he was commanded. And in Matthew 2:19-22, after being in Egypt some time hiding out from Herod, an angel of the Lord appeared again and told him to take the child back to Israel. Again, he got up and *took* the child back as he was commanded.

As I stated, Advent's invisible man didn't do that much but he was a man of action. The scriptures do not record all the deeds of

Joseph, but it is clear that his three responses were the most important acts in all of scripture. Perhaps they were the three most important acts in history. Had he failed to act, Jesus' life would have been jeopardized if not annihilated.

Sometimes it's not the amount of things that we do, but *that* we do something when the moment requires it. Failing to take action at critical times can cost us much. Joseph didn't pass decrees and implement legislation. He wasn't known for the enormity of his deeds, but the fact that he acted on the entreaties of God at a critical time makes him a man's man. In fact, after these critical actions, we seldom ever hear about Joseph again, but his actions saved humanity by allowing it to have a savior.

Think about it. He didn't have high visibility. In fact, we might say he had no visibility compared to others in the Bible. But he had three things which made him stand out. **He wasn't seen that much but he had substance. He wasn't heard that much but he had presence. He didn't do that much but he was a man of action.**

You don't have to be seen to be visible, just have substance in the things you have been called by God to do in your life. You don't have to be heard to have visibility, just have presence in all things vital. You don't have to do a lot to have visibility, just take action in times of critical decision making, and act decisively when the need arises.

Unlike H.G. Wells and Ralph Ellision's invisible men, Advent's "invisible man" changed the course of human history by playing a supporting role. By what he did, he allowed God to bring forth Jesus. Mary was a key player, but Joseph was behind the scenes. Invisibility does not mean lack of substance, lack of presence, or lack of action, just that God can still use someone of a low profile to do a great thing which can benefit the people of God.

Hang Time:
A Good Friday Sermon

Matthew 27:45-55

Lent is a season for recalling the suffering and triumph of our Lord, Savior and Liberator, Jesus Christ. It is a time where all Christians should take spiritual inventory in their lives; a time of discarding those things which hurt us and holding on to those things which help us. Lent is a time of remembering the passion, suffering, and resurrection of Christ. As heirs of his kingdom, we become co-participants in the struggle for love, justice, and truth as we are crucified and resurrected in the daily experiences of our lives.

It is interesting that a season of suffering should be the high point of our religious festivities. We are reminded that suffering has a central role in Christian experience, especially redemptive suffering. Suffering which brings about a new consciousness; a new relationship with God; a new awareness of our own spiritual power and God's ability to deliver us. The problem is most Christians want the crown of Christ without the cross of Christ. They want all the accolades and laurel wreaths of Christian pomp and pageantry but don't want to pay the price which goes with claiming the victory. They want the resurrection without the crucifixion. They want to be card-carrying members of the Christian faith but don't want to pay dues.

Being a Christian means that because Christ has suffered death on the cross for our redemption and liberation we should understand the why, what, and how of human suffering. If Christians don't understand anything else, they should at least know the meaning of redemptive suffering. How can we claim to have knowledge of the central and most important precepts of the Christian faith when we are afraid of the suffering and the pain which often

35

abides with it? We must deal with pain and suffering and summon the strength to do the right thing in all things even if it means ostracism and death.

Standing up for right often means pain, pain of rejection and persecution, and developing a willingness to suffer to bring about redemption.

Being Christian means you have come to terms with the suffering of Christ and the suffering of your own life. But Christians can't understand redemptive suffering until we fathom Jesus' hanging on the cross; how and why he hung will give us a clue to how we are able to hang through the tough times of our lives. Our theme this morning is "Hang Time": How long can you hang for the things that are of and for Christ? If he hung for us that we might have a better life, how are we hanging for him in making someone else's life better and the world a place of salvation and redemption? How are we hanging for Jesus? Are we hanging in or hanging out? What is our hang time for the things of God?

But before dealing with the Hang Time of Christ, we must deal with the **show time** of Passion Sunday and the **Hammer Time** of Good Friday.

For Judas and others Passion or Palm Sunday would be **show time**: a time when Jesus would ride into Jerusalem, brandishing swords on a white horse to usher in the new kingdom according to Jewish tradition. There were those who thought that Palm Sunday would be show time, a time for pageantry and pomp, a time of balloons, fireworks and confetti, and they were disappointed when Jesus rode in on a donkey without the dazzle, frazzle, and spectacle of such events.

There are many show time Christians. They hang only for a minute and then they're gone. When the show is over they hit the road. They're drawn to the Christian faith because of its glitter, its glamour; because it smacks of Fifth Avenue sensationalism. So long as the lights are shining and the bugles are blowing, so long as the banners are waving and the troops are marching, they're there for the show. These are show time individuals, sky-rocket Christians. Like the blaze of the rockets' red glare, they flash for a moment across the canopy of creation, then expend their light.

36

They like the show, but when there's work they are nowhere to be found. So long as the banners are streaming, the kites flying, the lights beaming, the crowds screaming, you can find them at center stage sucking up all the atmosphere, draining the coffers of human enthusiasm dry. Their presence is predictable. When there's a show, they show up; when there's work, they go home.

Some of them lined the streets of Jerusalem that Palm Sunday. Some of them attend churches today for the wrong reasons. It's all for show; it's all for status; it's all based on cheap grace: something for nothing theology. Many of them don't even pay when they show. They just specialize in showing up. They heard someone mention the word "free" and they show. They're worse than those who don't show and still pay.

One local pastor complained that his congregation lacked spiritual depth. That when it came to doing those things which were spiritually appropriate the people always complained and balked. This is interesting, he said. "Whenever it comes to doing things which are *spiritually correct*, I always have a problem. But when it comes to the things which are show oriented, I never have a problem. Something is wrong, Stewart. I have a lot of show time people in my church and this troubles me very much."

This preacher is not alone in his struggle. There are numerous others struggling with the same problems and difficulties — getting the people of God to become spiritually, instead of worldly, focused. This is not only a problem confronting Jesus on the streets of Jerusalem on Palm Sunday, but a malady plaguing our churches today. People want to be entertained but don't want to pay the admission price to building and sustaining, working and suffering for the kingdom of God.

While attracted to the glitter of church life, they circumspectly avoid the grime which goes with helping a church succeed and develop a winning attitude over the long haul. **Show time persons hang for the real things of Jesus for a little while**. Their hang time is nominal. They don't hang around for things in the Church that are of true spiritual value, nor do they hang in there when the going gets tough.

Second, there are the **Hammer Time** Christians. Another aspect of Lent besides Palm Sunday is the crucifixion of which I spoke earlier. The hammer time Christians show up for two reasons: to build up or to tear down; to crucify or to resurrect. There were those whose hammer time was spent nailing Jesus to the cross. Then there were those whose hammer time was spent making him a coffin so he would have a grave to lay in.

You can always trust the negative hammer time Christians to show up when a hanging or lynching is going on. They always have their hammers and nails and two-by-fours ready to nail somebody to the cross. Never mind that the person is good. Never mind that the person is innocent. Never mind they don't know the person. They always show up at hammer time, when it's time to nail somebody or tear somebody down. They never have a good thing to say about anybody. They are always criticizing and signifying in order to tear down. They can give less than a hoot about anybody else's feelings. They don't care one way or the other. When there's a lynching or a hanging, you can trust they'll always show up.

Perhaps three quarters of the folk who showed up for Jesus' crucifixion didn't know why they were there. The majority of those participating in his assassination only went on what others told them about him. These are the hammer time "Christians."

In my reading of the history of the old West, one writer said that because of the absence of social outlets and activities many people on the frontier showed up at hangings. These were often social events that the entire family came out to witness. They would bring their picnic baskets and Kool-Aid, make nice blanket pallets on the ground, watch the hanging, and then go home. Their greatest desire in life was to watch a hanging and go home. Some Christians are the same way, only they build the gallows, they pronounce the sentence, and they pull the cord leading to the scaffold. Their entire lives are spent living between Golgotha and Calvary instead of Calvary and Resurrection cemetery. They specialize not in hanging in for the things of Christ or hanging on to the joy of his promises, but hanging others for doing what's right.

38

These Hammer Time Christians, and I don't mean M.C. Hammer but J.C. Hammer, destroy anything that has to do with Jesus Christ: doing the right thing in his name; building his kingdom; serving his people; affirming his glory. They show up with their hammers and nails, ready to tear down and destroy. Such persons have always perplexed and baffled me, for the same energy they utilize in tearing things down can be sublimated into building God's kingdom. They're never on God's agenda. They are always running a personal agenda in the name of God. You can always tell where they've been, for they invariably leave a trail of blood, heartache, and heartbreak in their wake.

One writer said that there is much value in having these persons around. He says they remind us how ugly and cruel the world can be and tell us that the church is not exempt from the presence of evil. I understand this point and it is well taken, but I don't need to be reminded by hammer time people how cruel life can be. I am intimately aware through my own life struggles of how tough life can be. I see it every day when I read the newspapers or watch television or listen to the radio. What we need is people who will help build God's kingdom, spread his joy, provide some hallelujah hope for people in need. I'm not interested in folk who specialize in blowing other people's candles out but in those who know how to light a candle rather than curse the darkness and make the world a better place to live in.

Every Christian should be striving to make the world a better place to live in before he dies. If he's not doing that he's not paying his rent, as my late grandmother used to say. Everybody should be paying the rent here on earth by making the world a better place to live, and that's what Jesus was all about. But the hammer time folk tried to stop him dead in his tracks with some nine-inch nails and some two-by-fours and some cast iron hammers. Just as the show time people specialize in hanging for the things of Jesus for a short while, the hammer time people don't hang for the things of Jesus at all. They come with their nails and hammers and do their dirt, then go home. Theirs is no mission of mercy, but a mission of mess.

There is something within human nature, the human personality, that gravitates toward and relishes in the darker side of life: those things which reek of the tragic and the disconcerting. We must all struggle at some point or another not to allow this darker side to take us over so that we become the embodiment of bad news or the instruments of evil and destruction. We must fight daily not to get caught in the whirlwind of wrongdoing and strife, where the innocent are persecuted and the guilty are set free. We must all struggle not to become hammer time individuals wherein we woefully lament the good things of life and disparage those things which are truly of God.

As stated earlier, the show time people have a short hang time. The hammer time people have no hang time at all. They are not even remotely interested in building the kingdom of God and sharing the good news of Christ.

The third group is the **Hang Time Christians**. These are the people who hang in there for Christ. They even pay a price through personal suffering for the things that are of God.

You ever see Michael Jordan go to the hoop? He has rewritten the definition of hang time in the NBA. He hangs so long in the air before making his slam dunk that it's unbelievable. You know that the longer he hangs the more likely he'll score. The same is true of Christians who truly love and serve the Lord. They will score points on the scoreboard of eternity because they are part of a winning team, and they are willing to hang for as long as it takes to get the job done!

Jesus rewrote the book on hang time on the cross. Remember that the crucifixion and resurrection are two of the most important events in the Christian faith. The scriptures say that Jesus hung on the cross from the third to the ninth hour. He hung for us, that we might have a better life. He hung for truth that we might come to know it. He hung for justice that those who are unduly persecuted and incarcerated may be spiritually set free. He hung for love so that we could know that there is a better, higher way in living our lives. Jesus rewrote the definition of hang time. He hung longer than anyone else before him for our liberation and salvation.

We must remember that crucifixion was a terrible mode of execution and death. It was perhaps imported from Carthage, but was used regularly by Rome as a means of executing criminals and insurrectionists. I say that it was a terrible mode of death because the individual would hang for long hours until the weight of his body suffocated him to death. Besides the pain inflicted by the nails and hammers, the weight of the body created excruciating agony for the person.

To think that Jesus paid this price for us is the source of our hope and joy! It was his hang time on the cross which is the basis of his sacrifice for us. It was his hang time on the cross that serves as an offering for our salvation. It was his hang time on the cross that makes a difference in our spiritual lives today!

Accordingly, it is our hang time for the things of God, for love, truth, justice, salvation, and liberation of the people of God, which makes the qualitative spiritual difference in our lives. It is not the show time which defines us, not the hammer time which describes us, but the hang time which saves us.

What is your hang time? Can you hang in there for Christ in the midst of persecution? Can you hang for those things which promote and help build the kingdom of God? Can you hang for Jesus? How long can you hang? What is your hang time for the things of God?

I think about all those faithful servants of Christ who are able to hang in a mighty way. They're able to hang in there for Jesus when everybody else is abandoning ship. Their staying power is beyond belief. It was the hang time or staying power of the church in the midst of persecution and hardship that allows us to be here today. It was the hang time or staying power of the martyrs and early Christians which brought us the gifts of the church we now enjoy. Hang time is the time we spend sacrificing ourselves for the things of God in the midst of personal suffering and life's seemingly insurmountable difficulties. The longer we hang for Jesus, the better life becomes for the people of God!

Christ gives us a staying power and ability to hang through the tough times by his sacrifice on the cross. By hanging for us, and by following and accepting him, we are able to hang through the tough times of our lives.

We all lament the passing of our dear brother Charles Garner on yesterday morning. We will miss Charles and all the gifts and joy he brought to Hope through his music. He hung in there during a time in our ministry when we needed new guidance and direction, when our program needed help. Charles left a larger church to come to Hope church, and we appreciate his hanging in there to make our lives better through his music ministry.

In the end he hung on as long as he could. He hung for the things of God by trying to do the right thing. Charles was a good man. His hang time was tremendous. We know in the latter days how painful it was for him. But he said, "I've got to get back to my music. I've got to get back to Hope church." Despite his personal pain and suffering he hung in there for the Lord!

Oh, how often are we distracted by the pain and suffering? How often will the least little thing prevent us from going on to greater heights and glory? Many people shouted at Jesus to come down from the cross to save himself. But he was determined to hang in there for his people. Determined to pay the price for our liberation and redemption. Thank God for the hang time of Jesus.

What is your hang time today? Do you feel discouraged? Are you ready to give up hope and trust in God's ability to deliver you from defeat and despair? What is your hang time today? Is it six seconds or six years? How much are you willing to pay to build the kingdom of God? How much are you willing to sacrifice to make your life and those around you better than you found it? Your hang time will give you a clue to your staying power for the things that are of God. Hang in there! Whatever you're facing, hang in there, for God will see you through!

Fatal Subtraction

Acts 4:32—5:11

Today I want to revisit a sermon preached some years ago titled "Fatal Subtraction." Based on the Acts 4 and 5 scriptures of Ananias and Sapphira, it centers on the story of a husband and wife who took away things from their lives and ended up dead. Theirs was a fatal subtraction because they subtracted where they were supposed to add and added where they were supposed to subtract. It is clear they had not mastered the basic principles of Christian arithmetic and died because they held back a vital portion of their earnings which were promised to the church. They reduced their gifts during a critical time of the early church and threatened to undermine its forward movement.

Our story today finds Peter and the other apostles working hard to spread the Good News of the risen Christ. They have boldly stood before their adversaries and renounced the decadence and power of Satan. The new movement of the followers of the way is gaining momentum as more people are converted to the faith.

The Church is in infancy. It is a time of great struggle. It is a time of great crisis. The work conducted by the apostles during this time would be the litmus test of the new faith. If they could succeed in winning new persons to Christ, they would have a solid foundation to build a Church for the future, one which would be an enduring legacy to the living Christ. Whatever they did now, they would have to go all out. Give their all and best to build the Church of Christ.

Each person joining the church understood the value and importance of supporting its mission. Early Christians believed that God called them for the noble purpose of building a new spiritual consciousness which would place the Church at the center of earthly activities. Whenever new persons converted to Christ, it was understood that they would give what they vowed to support the church's ministry. In his book *Property and Riches in The Early Church*, scholar Martin Hengel observes that all goods and property were held in common so no needs were unmet in those early Christian communities. So it was clearly understood by new believers that they would have to support wholly and joyfully the mission of the Church's survival and expansion once they accepted Christ. (It wasn't like today where what membership means for some is a loosely defined set of propositions.)

Then come Ananias and Sapphira. They were wealthy landowners who joined the church. They promised to give all they had for the glory of Christ and the preservation of the Church, but they held back. They subtracted when they were supposed to add and imperiled the entire community by their selfish actions. The Church was trying to move forward but they threatened to stymie its progress through their own greed.

The scriptures say that Ananias sold a piece of property and held back a portion of the profit. He could have kept some profit for himself. There was nothing saying he had to give all the profit to the church. His problem was that he lied to God, the Holy Spirit and Peter and the other apostles. When Peter asked him if he turned in all his earnings he said, "Yes," knowing he was lying. At that moment he was struck down and died because he lied to God — blasphemed the Holy Spirit by not keeping the promise he made to God when he joined the Church.

His wife came shortly thereafter and she, too, was asked by Peter the same question. And she, too, was struck down by the Spirit and died because she lied about her earnings.

Now this may seem to be cruel to some. That their subtraction from God should be fatal seems a very curious thing. However, when we look more closely at the meaning of their membership in the early Church, we understand more fully why they met such a fate.

We must understand that in joining the church they were committing themselves to the first law of spirituality from a Christian viewpoint, and that law is: I will do all I can and give all I can to help spread the word and ministry of Christ through his church. The first law of spirituality, which is the foundation of all Christian commitment, is **giving**.

So first, **they violated the principle of giving by holding back a portion of their wealth**.

You cannot be a thoroughbred Christian unless you are willing to give of yourself, time and treasure for building God's church. Everything in the church revolves around the first principle of giving. If you are not giving something to your church you are violating the first law of spirituality.

Look in the beginning. Here God gave us creation. God gave us the world: the earth, the sky, the sea, the wind, the sun, and the rain. God gave first before God did anything else. God gave first of him/herself. God created all that is, which means that God brought his/her creative energy to fruition by creating material substances which form the foundation of the universe. In creating humankind, God gave to man God's very own breath and made him in God's very own image. God's first act of creation was to give us something we could have life on and life through. We have life on earth and life through Christ and we would have had neither had God not given. We cannot understand the primordial workings of God in creation without understanding the dynamics of giving, which is the first principle of life and spirituality.

How then do we sustain this life? By giving of themselves in love and procreation, man and woman perpetuate life. We could not have life's continuation without man and woman giving of themselves in love for the purpose of perpetuating humankind.

The most important acts of creation revolve around the principle of giving. Even better, in John 3:16, we find an even deeper testimony. "God so loved that world that He *gave* his only son and whosoever believeth in him shall not perish but have everlasting life." Again the first principle of giving is manifested by God in offering us Christ.

So what made Ananias and Sapphira's sin so detrimental is that they violated the first law of spirituality, and that is giving something of value for the succession of God's church. By joining the church they made a commitment to give, but they held back and lied about their gifts, which led to their tragic demise. Their error was doubly sorry because it was done during a time when the church really needed them to be faithful and honest about their commitment to Christ. It's similar to people who have joined the church today, committed themselves to give to the church and then don't give because of apathy, stinginess, and selfishness. They can give something, but refuse at a critical time of the church's journey.

Here I am not referring to people who simply don't have it and can't give it. I'm talking about people who have it and refuse to give it because they don't take God, the church, and their commitment seriously. They are playing a dangerous game of fatal subtraction. They would be better off not making a commitment than playing the dangerous game of Christian roulette.

In recently surveying our Capital Funds Campaign commitments, I am pleased and thank God for the people who have given to this worthy effort. I am pleased that there are people who haven't pledged but have still managed to give something. And again, it's not the amount, but the sacrifice. But I am thoroughly baffled by the people who call themselves members of this church who have given not one red cent to this effort, but call themselves committed Christians. Who are they fooling? Certainly not God! It's not that they can't give. It's that they won't give, and this is certainly a disgrace to God and the church and is clearly a violation of the first principle of spirituality. Now there are some waiting to give. I understand that. Some who don't know about our campaign and would like to hear more before they give. But those who know and are not planning to give out of selfishness hinder the church's progress.

You can't call yourself a member in good standing when there is zero by your name in the giving column. There is no excuse for not giving at least a penny to the Lord's work. In the area of financial giving there should never be a zero by someone's name, because if you can't tithe, you give something, even if it is a nickel, a dime, or a quarter or half-dollar.

Ananias and Sapphira's crime is that they practiced cheap grace and fibbed about it all in one roll. It's almost equivalent to refusing to give a hungry baby badly needed milk. That milk is essential to the survival of the baby, but we refuse to give it what it needs out of our own sin and selfishness. The money they held back was critical to the survival of the church.

Secondly, **they not only violated the principle of giving but also placed the entire community in jeopardy by their refusal to give**. Seldom do we think about how our actions impact those around us. Christians must understand that as the Body of believers we're not in this thing by ourselves but together. What one does affects all. What all do affect one. **The second law of spirituality is sharing in community**. If giving is the act of surrendering something of value, sharing is the act of giving something of value so as to benefit others around you. By holding back and subtracting they threatened to destroy the body of Christ by refusing to share. Sharing sustains belief. Sharing creates fellowship. Sharing solidifies the body of believers. The church's success is based on a willingness to share.

Early believers knew that sharing empowered them to be more effective in reaching others for Christ. One writer observed that it was precisely their willingness to share all that attracted many followers to Christ. By refusing to share what they had, they threatened to destroy the moral and spiritual foundation of the church. If sharing is the spiritual glue which held people together after love brought them together, refusing to share would tear the glue apart.

Christians should give more thought to the long-term consequences of our actions. It is easy, tempting, to think selfishly. But giving to a worthy cause of Christ carries more than its weight in gold because our giving impacts others around us, either positively or negatively. People should seriously consider how their refusal to give to the church adversely impacts their church family. What made Ananias' and Sapphira's acts so critical was that they held back during a time when their giving would have made the most difference in helping God realize God's purpose through the church. Had they not promised to give, the results may have not been so devastating. What they did threatened to destroy the church's progress.

Finally, **their greed, selfishness, and covetousness prevented the Holy Spirit from doing its greatest work, which limited their testimony**. If we would only realize how we limit God, how we, through our refusal to give and to share, stifle the Holy Spirit.

Nothing discomfits God more than our refusal to keep our promise after joining God, our hard-heartedness in not doing the things that will help the church succeed.

I am continually amazed at the good talk people give about how good they are. They talk a good game, but all you have to do is look in the contribution column and see the number zero. I say, as I've said before, there is no excuse for anyone not giving something to the church. If a homeless man can walk into a church service and drop three pennies into the building fund offering, why can't those better off do better? We don't understand how we are blowing our blessing each day and dwarfing the Holy Spirit's effort to use us for the good of Christ.

Ananias and Sapphira turned away the Holy Spirit through selfishness and this was an abomination to God.

What they subtracted was fatal to themselves but nearly proved fatal to that early body of believers. What they did violated the first and second laws of spirituality, which are giving and sharing. It threatened to destroy the Body of Christ and prevent the Holy Spirit from using the people of God for the Glory of God. Where are you today? Where do you stand in the mix? Have you kept your promise to support the church in your membership vows or have you been tempted to hold back? Keep giving to the cause of Christ. Don't let the example of Ananias and Sapphira lure you into holding back on God when you should be giving all you have to build God's Kingdom and support God's Church.

Hostage Crisis

1 Kings 19:1-18; Luke 4:14-21

Sweat swarmed and beaded the palms of his hands as his heart thumped and pulse escalated. Bulging eyes blinked rapidly as his face twitched. His brown, swollen hands rumbled nervously through the inside pocket of his urine-stained tweed overcoat. "I got to find a match," he said to himself. "I got to find a match." Again he jerked through every pocket of his pants, jacket, and shirt. Still no match.

Wildly flailing his arms more frantically now, he began over-turning chairs and tables in the room. Yellow eyes widened in disbelief as he hunched his back Neanderthal-like in search of that fire; that flame to heat the cooker that would launch his mind, body, and soul beyond the confines of reality. "I got to find a match," he whispered, half screaming. "If I don't find that match, I'm gonna kill somebody!"

Finally, the match. Now the pipe and that little white ball of crack. Now he would take leave of his five senses. Now he would take refuge in that white ghost; the white witch that promised to be the answer to his deepest yearnings. Now he would do the solemn death dance and prepare himself to go as high and as far as the junk would take him.

The hostage crisis is not where terrorists, brandishing semi-automatic weapons, heap scorn and scourge upon the innocent by taking them captive. The hostage crisis is not where planes are skyjacked and trains derailed by perpetrators of the sabotage, making prisoners of the undeserving. It is not a crisis of oil, guns, bread or butter. It is not the public theater of disgrace, shame, and humiliation brought about by political insurrectionists and dissidents desiring to vault center stage to air their grievances. No, the hostage crisis I'm referring to today is none of these things.

The hostage crisis today is where the people of God are taken prisoner by evil and spiritual decadence, where souls have sold out to Satan; where the spiritually anointed are held captive by their own vices, devices, and perverse longings. It is a crisis of flesh and blood, of fear and trembling; a failure of nerve; where the things of God that are good are warring to prevent the things that are of Satan from taking over their minds and souls. The hostage crisis we face today is far greater than any political act of terrorism, for it is a crisis which compromises the will and plan of God for our lives. It is crisis which alienates, degrades, and destroys well-meaning, good-intentioned people.

Everywhere we look we see evidence of this crisis. People punished and persecuted for doing the right thing, for exemplifying all that is good and right and just. The crisis is one where good is held hostage to evil; where the innocent suffer at the hands of the deceitful and diabolical; where people desiring to live forthright and upstanding lives are made prisoners of fear, uncertainty, and loss of hope and faith in the power of God to transcend and deliver them. This is a crisis of great magnitude, for Satan is at war to make hostages of the people of God; to bind them so they can't do the Lord's work; to intimidate, discourage, alienate, and obliterate God's plan for the redemption of God's people.

We don't have to look to headlines to see a hostage crisis. We see it every day where people are given life sentences in four-by-four cells of shame, fear, self-hatred, and self-destruction, so that their lives are lived within the solitary confines of despair and grief. The hostage crisis is everywhere. In our homes, in the church, on our jobs, in the schools, in the hallowed halls of government. Wherever the people of God are not free to live wholesome, productive, and spirit-filled lives for fear of repression and repercussion is a hostage crisis. The weapons used to destroy and intimidate are not AK-47's, but weapons designed to dash the spirit and defuse the joy for Christ of the people of God.

Three basic things lead to hostage situations in the people of God. First is loss of faith in God's ability to deliver. Second is fear of reprisals and repercussion for doing the things of God, and third is outright ignorance to the best laid plans of God for us.

We see in our scripture lesson today a classic case of spiritual hostage taking. Elijah, called by God, is put on the run by Jezebel and Ahab. After challenging the prophets of Baal and destroying them, Jezebel issues a death threat which sends Elijah fleeing for his life. Before, when of God, he was a spiritually free man. We see him standing boldly on Mount Carmel denouncing the gods of Baal and their pagan blood rites. He is the man of the hour, claiming his mountain as a fortress for the God of Israel.

He is undaunted, undashed, and undenuded. He stands strongly as a man of God, confident in God's power to save, redeem, and deliver. But after destroying the prophets of Baal, we find in 1 Kings 19:2 and 3:

> So Jezebel sent a messenger to Elijah to say, "May the gods deal with me, be it ever so severely, if by this time tomorrow I do not make your life like that of one of them." Elijah was afraid and ran for his life.

At first he was a spiritually free man, but now he was a hostage of fear. Jezebel and Ahab put him on the run and the scriptures say that Elijah was so afraid, he hid out in a cave in fear for his life.

Before — a bastion of courage. Now — a hostage of fear. So scared was he that he wished he would die. Fear prompted him to thoughts of suicide. Confident he was one moment, suicidal he was the next.

See him now hiding out in a cave. What cowardice! One moment, standing on Mount Carmel having a mountaintop experience. The next moment he is hiding in a cave. From a mountain of courage to a cave of fear goes Elijah.

How often do we find ourselves as the people of God in similar situations? At times we are so armed with the confidence of God that no one and no thing can move us from our mountain. Then someone issues the threat and we're hostages hiding in fear. In the first instance we take no prisoners. In the next instant we are the prisoner. Fear becomes our jailer and the fugitive way is our life sentence. Elijah ran. How often do we run? Hostages running from the truth. Hostages running in fear. Hostages running to be running, not knowing where we're running to and who we're running from.

The great writer Richard Wright in his celebrated classic *Native Son* tells the story of Bigger Thomas who runs from the law because he accidentally kills the daughter of his employer. Bigger is a hostage of fear, escaping the haunting truth of a past crime. But in a larger sense, Bigger is running from a central truth of his existence. He is a prisoner of self-doubt all along. He never comes to realize his potential and worth as a person because of the fear instilled within him at birth. He may have articulated the fear in those immortal words of Shakespeare's Hamlet, "To be or not to be. That is the question...." Or who can forget Raskolnikov in Dostoyevsky's *Crime and Punishment*, who kills the old pawnbroker and thus too becomes a hostage of his own sin, as he constantly wars with his own flesh and spirit? Dostoyevsky's masterpiece is a commentary on the spiritual struggles of humankind, the war of the spiritual and material; man's longing to transcend the hostage situations which bind and seduce him and forever take his sanity, well-being and peace. His imprisonment stems from not doing the right thing, knowing all along it is the thing to do.

Elijah is hostage to fear. It is a fear induced by a crisis in faith. Somewhere between Mount Carmel and Mount Horeb, between Mount Horeb and the cave, he lost confidence in God. Before he was strong, and now he is weak.

Whatever holds us hostage, we can trace its origins to a crisis in confidence, where we no longer hold fast to our faith in God's ability to redeem and deliver. Every spiritual crisis culminating in our spiritual incarceration is due to lack of belief in God. It is only by retrieving our faith and trust that we are able to bust out of our spiritual jail cells and knock down the walls which close us in.

All along the way God is giving Elijah encouragement to rebuild his confidence. God gives him cakes of bread to feed his hunger and jars of water to quench his thirst. Even as a hostage, God provides Elijah with the necessities to survive and break free.

Isn't that just like God? Whenever we need God most, God is there to loosen the chains, setting us spiritually free. God can make you free again, only you must trust in God's Word and heed God's voice as God calls unto you.

Elijah is a hostage to fear, but God all along is giving him the keys to get out of jail. Elijah's fear is because he has lost faith.

Second, **Elijah is held hostage by ignorance**. After being placed on the run and hiding out, he discovers that God had provided seven thousand reserves in Israel whose knees have not bowed to Baal and whose mouths have not kissed him. Elijah was ignorant of this fact, but had he kept his faith and confidence in God, he would have known that God had a backup, some prayer warriors praying prayers of deliverance. Had he not allowed his ignorance to lock him up and throw away the key, he could have broken free immediately. Ignorance of how, when, and why God works can bind like no terrorist ever can. If you're ignorant of the Word, ignorant of God's will, ignorant of how God's Holy Spirit works, you're nothing but a potential hostage for Satan and his legions.

Elijah's fear led to ignorance and ignorance led to his further spiritual incarceration and disintegration. But God's got an answer for Elijah.

God says to him in verses 9-11: "And the *Word* of the Lord came to him. Elijah, what are you doing here? Go stand on the mountain in the presence of the Lord because the Lord is about to pass by."

His ignorance of the Word coupled with his own crisis of faith had made him a hostage of fear and ignorance. Now that the Word had come to him he was back on his way to spiritual freedom, no longer held hostage.

So he went and stood on the mountain. God made him do the very thing which is symbolic of spiritual freedom, standing on the mountain, trusting in the Lord, being guided by God's Spirit and delivered through God's Word. So Elijah stands there, a free man once again, because the Word of God has come to give confidence; to unbind the fear and loose the ignorance that had held him hostage.

He's a free man now. Why free? Because he was open to God's word of deliverance and obediently responded to God's commands. You still a hostage? Read the word of God. You still a prisoner? Heed God's holy Word! You still shut up, bound up and tied up? Put your hand in his hand and trust in God to deliver you.

Before, he was hostage to fear and ignorance because of a crisis of faith, now he was free again because the Word of God came to him and he obediently responded to God's word.

Why is the hostage crisis still going on? Because we've had a crisis of faith, because fear and ignorance have taken us over. The Word is a liberating word. Had Elijah kept it in the hollow of his heart, Ahab and Jezebel couldn't have put him on the run. Had he known the prayer warriors were praying and the saints of God were staying on his side, he could have stayed on that mountain and put the king and queen on the run by the wrath of God. If he could stand up to the prophets of Baal, why not Ahab and Jezebel?

Like Elijah, God can set you free! God set Jacob free. No longer a prisoner on the run. God set him free by God's Spirit. God set the Hebrews free from Egyptian bondage. God set Daniel free through the power of God's Spirit. Daniel was a prisoner of Babylon but was more free because he kept his faith and trust in the God of his fathers and mothers. God set Paul free on the Damascus Road. God set Jesus free to be the embodiment of the Word.

God can set you free by receiving God's Word through the power of the Holy Ghost.

Jesus says in Luke 4:18: "The Spirit of the Lord is upon me, because he has anointed me to preach the good news to the poor, to proclaim freedom for those who are bound up and recovery of sight to the blind, to set at liberty those who are oppressed, to proclaim the acceptable year of the Lord."

The junkie with the cooker at this sermon's opening is now a free man because he turned away from his sinful addiction and allowed the word of God to come into his life. And he discovered that the prayer saints never stopped praying. If Christ can free him from crack; if God freed Elijah from fear of Jezebel's traps, freed Jesus from the bonds of Satan's wraps, God can free you and

54

me from the chains of hopelessness and despair. If you're gonna be a prisoner, be a prisoner for Christ. If you're gonna be a slave, be a slave for Christ. If you're gonna be a terrorist, be a terrorist for Christ, but don't be held hostage out of fear and ignorance of the power of the Lord!

Break free from the chains of fear and annihilation! Break free from the chains of ignorance and despair! Break free from the four walls of addiction and self-destruction! Break free from those things which hold you hostage and prevent you from being all God wants you to be!

Break free from those solitary confinements, those mini-imprisonments which dash your desire to live freely and wholly in Christ!

Under New Management

2 Corinthians 5:14-21; 7:1-11

I'll call him Raj to protect his identity. Some of you may know him. I knew him very well. We went to junior high and high school together. He was an affable fellow who was very likable. He always had a good joke to tell and was full of the devil. He epitomized the phrase, "No fools, no fun." He was the life of the party and always a joy to be with. He was one of the best rappers in the world. People would gather round just to hear him rap, and anybody who went against him was always dead meat because he had the gift of gab that could blow anybody away. He was smooth and just the way he phrased a sentence would make you laugh your hat off.

I saw Raj about five years ago down at the Detroit Rescue mission. I was shocked to see him there. He looked old and tired. The glow was gone. The wide, toothy smile had long since disappeared. There were no jokes to tell, no laughter to punctuate our conversation. No signifying, dozens or name-calling. I saw him in the food line wearing a long, grey, urine-stained overcoat, combat boots, and glasses that had only one stem across his right ear. When our eyes met I could gather a sense of joy and sadness. "Stew," he said, "what's up man? Long time no see. How you been? What you doing down here?" We embraced. I could smell the urine, the smell of stale alcohol on his breath as we shook hands.

"I came down as part of my ministry. I am in the ministry now, Raj." He gave me that you-got-to-be-jiving half-grin, looking at me sideways.

"Man, I knew you was going to do something. But the ministry? I guess you didn't have a choice. Everybody in your family was preachers. Wasn't your mama a preacher, too?" he said, snickering and slowly coming to life.

"Man, you know my mama wasn't no preacher." We both laughed.

"What happened, Raj? How did you end up here in the mission?" I asked plaintively.

"It's a long story. You got a minute? Let's rap."

We sat down and talked a long time. Raj's story was truly one of bad luck. If anybody had a hard luck story it was Raj. He had gone away to Michigan State University after high school. His mother was killed by burglars breaking into her home when he was a junior at State. His father became an alcoholic. His youngest brother was killed dealing drugs and his oldest sister was shot in the head by a jealous boyfriend.

Raj was the oldest of six children and the only one who went to college to make something out of himself. He graduated from Michigan State with a bachelor's degree in business and finance. After leaving State, he had a hard time finding a job. He worked at the post office for a short stint and did odd jobs to make ends meet. He had worked hard at State, graduating with a B average, but still could find no work after graduation. He finally got a job with an accounting firm, but the owner was indicted for misappropriation of funds and the company folded.

Things began to get better when he met his soon-to-be wife Betty. Betty had a good paying job as a registered nurse at a local hospital. They got married and had four children. Shortly after marriage, Raj got a good paying job as the manager of an apartment complex. He was given a lush, palatial crib on the premises and the work was people work, which he liked very much. He was manager of the "Shady Rest" apartment complex and living on Easy Street. He didn't pay rent. All his lights, gas, and other utilities were paid by the owner of the complex. He could come and go as he pleased and got a bonus if he got exceptionally good tenants to live on the premises.

Raj was a good public relations representative. He could talk and talk. He would take prospective tenants on tours of the complex and discuss the advantages of living in such a wonderful place. In ninety percent of his cases the persons chose to live at his complex. Raj cared about his tenants and did all he could to meet their needs. He was an honest, hard-working individual who went out of his way to make sure the tenants were pleased.

"Stew, I was living good. The landlord was great. The pay was great. The ambience was great. The terms and benefits of the job were great, and all I had to do was manage the place and make sure that all the amenities were up to snuff and in good working order. It was like heaven. Betty and I could save some money because we didn't have to pay rent. The kids could use the playground facilities in the complex and the place was very safe. I loved being the manager of that place. It was the best job I ever had. I had total peace of mind being a manager, the head negro in charge.

"Then one day it all fell apart, man. Betty up and left and took the kids with her. She met some doctor in the hospital who blew her mind and the next thing I knew she said she didn't love me any more and was gone. Just like that. In a twinkling of an eye. One minute we were deeply in love and the next minute she's off with some doctor dude. That really broke my heart, man. She is the only woman I really ever loved.

"It all began to fall apart for me then, man.

"My oldest son got involved with the wrong crowd some years later and got shot and killed, mistaken for somebody else. I feel so angry because I never knew what really happened. Betty wouldn't tell me what happened and getting information was like pulling wisdom teeth. My oldest girl got pregnant and won't speak to me or her mama. Several years ago I was diagnosed with a brain tumor because I was having all these headaches. I went in for surgery and they say they got all the tumor and I haven't had problems since. The problem is when I went into convalescence for the cancer, I lost my job at the apartment complex. Can you believe that, man? After all the years I gave to that place as the manager, the best manager they ever had, they decided to terminate me because of an illness I couldn't help. Can you believe they did that to me?

"So, man, I lost everything. I lost my job. I lost my wife and children. I nearly lost my life to cancer and so I ended up here at the Mission. I've been homeless for three years, man, without work, without self-esteem and with no place to rest my head. I thought about killing myself so many times it ain't funny. I got a degree but can't find a job. The previous landlord who owned the apartments died of a heart attack and I can't even get a decent reference for twelve years of my life so I can get a good-paying job. Every place I've been they say I'm either too old, I don't have enough experience or the wrong degree in the wrong area. It's always an excuse not to hire me and it just makes me mad. Now, I don't even have a decent stitch of clothing so I can go on a job interview."

We talked a long time into the night. Hours passed as Raj poured out his heart and soul. I told him I would do everything I could to help him. He cried. I cried. We had prayer. I put my last forty dollars in his top shirt pocket as I left and promised to come back down to the mission that Friday with some concrete plans to get him out of that place. It was a blue Monday if ever there was one and I was thoroughly depressed when I walked out of that mission.

When I returned home I vowed to leave no stone unturned in helping Raj out of his situation. I would pull some strings, get on the phone, and see if I could find him a job somewhere until he could get on his feet. I began to appreciate my own suffering more. There's always someone worse off and we should always, always, always count our blessings. When I returned on Friday, like I promised, Raj was long gone. I called him Tuesday, Wednesday, and Thursday to keep contact with him and he said he would be waiting for me. Some people said that he left that Thursday and hadn't seen him since. The next several months I combed the streets looking for Raj. I searched the streets of the Cass corridor, up and down Woodward Avenue. I searched high and low looking for Raj. No Raj. I went back to the mission many times since and he never came back. Needless to say, I was very disappointed.

I had gotten some commitments from a few people to help the man. Employment, even a temporary place to stay where he would have three hots and a cot, but no Raj. The last time I saw Raj was in 1990, five years ago, after putting forty dollars in his pocket and walking out of the mission. I have always wondered what happened to him. I would even cruise down his old street, Montgomery, to see if I might catch sight of him. No Raj. He disappeared. Out of sight, but not out of my mind.

Why would this man who had every opportunity to get help disappear like that? Was it the alcohol? Was it his heartache and heartbreak? Was he embarrassed that I saw him in that condition? No shame for me, knowing I've always been two or three paychecks from the bread line myself! Did he kill himself? Was he in jail or prison? Did he kill someone else and do some time? How could he vanish like that, knowing I was coming to the rescue?

Needless to say, I gave up my search for Raj. I accepted that I would never find or see him again. But God works not only in mysterious ways, but mischievous ways. One day as I was standing in the car wash making sure that my car was getting the treatments I paid for, someone tapped me on the shoulder. When I turned around, I couldn't believe my eyes. It was Raj, standing there with that wide, toothy grin, smelling all fresh with Chanel, decked out in an olive green double-breasted suit, with a green tie, black alligator shoes, and a beige trench coat, with his Stetson cocked ace deuce, clean as a whistle, with a new look and a new attitude.

"Hey man, what's going on?" I shouted as we laughed and embraced. "I've been looking for you for the last five years, man. What happened? Why did you dis me that way and disappear? I've been looking everywhere for you and couldn't find you nowhere. I had a job and everything waiting for you, man...."

"I know, Stew, but I had to get out of Dodge," he said abruptly. "I took that forty dollars along with twenty-five I had and caught the first Greyhound bus to Cleveland to stay with my sister to get myself together, man. I kept thinking the whole time we was talking, man. I kept looking at you, how far you had come and the great things you were doing and talking about, man. I kept thinking that after all the things I had, being the manager of an apartment, going to college and getting my degree, getting married, having and raising my children. After all that, man, and after my conversation with you, I realized there was one thing missing in my life, man, and that was Jesus Christ. I kept thinking I didn't have Christ in my life. Yes, I had material things but I didn't have Christ. Yes, I had an education, but I didn't have Christ. Yes, I had a wife and a family, but we didn't have Christ. It was the way you witnessed to me, man, about what Christ had done in your life. I could see what Christ was doing for you, so I had to get myself together by turning my life over to Christ.

"I used to be the manager of an apartment complex, but I want to tell you, Stew, that I'm under new management now. I got a new life now. I got a new landlord now, Stew. My life has changed since I found Christ."

He referred to 2 Corinthians 5:17: *"Therefore if anyone is in Christ, he is a new creation. The old has gone and the new has come."* (NIV)

"I used to worry about having a place in Mr. Robinson's apartment house. Now I know I have a place in my father's house. Mr. Robinson used to be my landlord. My new landlord is Christ Jesus. There are no For Sale signs marked out front of my Father's house. Just,'**All are Welcome and anybody who enters will be remade like new**.'

"I used to worry about short-term leases, now I have a long-term eternal lease through Christ Jesus. I don't fret about who owns the property. Jesus has the title to my property.

"I used to worry about keys to the apartments of Mr. Robinson's place, now I have the keys to God's Kingdom. The old keys would rust and fade. I would have to change the locks and get new keys made for the various tenants. The keys to the kingdom never rust, never fade, never have to be remade to fit the lock. I don't call Mr. Goodlock. I have keyless entry to the kingdom through Christ. I call Mr. Gooddoor who opens doors no man can shut and shuts doors no man can open!

"I used to worry about no-knock laws in the apartments. But in my Father's house it says, 'Knock and it shall be opened to you, seek and you shall find, ask and it shall be given unto you.'

62

"I used to worry about security deposits, now under God's salvation plan the deposit has already been made through the sacrifice of Christ Jesus. I don't worry about security deposits because He's already paid up, already paid the price by giving his life. I have security. I don't need to deposit. I don't need to worry about putting up a finder's fee. I've already been found. I've already been saved. My security has already been bought and paid for through Christ Jesus.

"I used to worry about the interior decorators in the apartment complex. Now I got a new interior decorator who has refurbished the walls and floors, the cabinets and doors of my new house with love, joy, forgiveness, and reconciliation. I'm under new management now. Christ is the head of my life. When Satan came to claim me in a final effort to win my soul, Jesus showed up with a quick claim deed, claiming me as His own.

"I don't give overdue notices or shut off notices. I don't receive damage deposits. There's repentance, mercy, hallelujah love, hallelujah joy, forgiveness, reconciliation, holiness, and justification by faith. I don't get notices from the utility companies. I don't have a light bill; I just walk in the light of Christ Jesus, Jerusalem Power and Light. I don't have a gas bill, no consumers' power, just Holy Ghost power!

"I'm under new management now. The old has passed away and the new creation has come through Christ. I have confessed Jesus Christ with my mouth and believe in Him by faith. I trust in Him.

"I walked the streets after we met and decided to give my life to Christ. That was the one thing missing, Stew, that I didn't have. I have prayed so much I have worn out pairs of pants at the knees. I'm under new management now. Betty's under new management now. My children are under new management now. I have a good paying job, I'm living in a decent neighborhood, and Christ is the head of my life. I got a new chairman of the board, a new president, a new board of directors, a new lease on life, a new opportunity to grow through Christ. Christ has made me new. All things old have passed away. Putting behind me the former things, I march on for the high prize of the calling of Christ Jesus. The rent has been paid. The ransom has been made. I'm under new management and I'm just so happy. Thank you for saving my life. Thank you for helping me to see the light of Christ."

Raj's story ends on a high note. But what about you today? Is it time for new management? Is it time to turn in that old lease and get a new lease on life? Is it time to move into your Father's house? Is it time to become a brand-new creation in Christ? Raj turned it over to Christ and that's what some of you need to do this morning. Turn it over. Wear that sign, "Under new management." God lives here. Under new management. No vacancies.

The point here is that Raj got saved. By being saved he was under new management. The important thing that Raj learned was not the house he lived in but who built the house, not how high those apartment complexes reached but who was the foundation. He was under new management because he got a new foundation for his life. Isaiah 28:16 (KJV) says: *"Behold I lay in Zion for a foundation, a stone, a tried stone, a precious cornerstone, a sure foundation. And 1 Corinthians 3:11: "For no other foundation can man lay than that which is laid, in Jesus Christ."* He was saved.

Raj was concerned about the outward things, but true power and new management of our lives come when we turn over the interior to Christ. He becomes our new interior decorator, putting salvation, mercy, reconciliation, and forgiveness as the new appointments in our Father's house. What is your foundation today? Are you resting on that solid rock? Do you need a new landlord who will give you a new lease on life?

That's what we need here at Hope Church. Christians who are saved, under new management where Christ is truly the head of our lives. We need new management, the new creation in Christ. We must therefore repent, confess, and profess our faith in Christ Jesus so that he can truly become the head of our lives. Who's in charge of your life? Who's your landlord? Who holds the title to your property? Who has your eternal deed in God's name? What keys are you using? What security deposits have you claimed? What "light" bill are you paying? What is your fuel source? On what foundation are you laid this morning? Is anybody truly home at your house? I'm under new management because Christ is now the head of my life!

Can You Dig It?

Genesis 26:1-31

Our scripture today finds Isaac, the son of Abraham, faced with the formidable task of holding his family together, restoring their spiritual legacy and vouchsafing their future amid death threats and vehement opposition from the Philistines. Isaac must decide whether to dig or not to dig the wells of his father and exalt his people to their rightful place in history or allow his adversaries and enemies to foil his plans.

The question for Isaac is: *Can he dig* the wells of hope, prosperity, and the restoration of his people's personhood and spirituality? For Isaac knew, as we know today, that *personhood* and spirituality go hand in hand, for as long as others have the power to define your personhood they have the power to spiritually define you as a non-person. And that's the problem with us today as a people. We have conferred on others the power to determine and define the worth, the depth, and the very trajectory of our being. Small wonder that spiritual dislocation has led to personal, communal, and familial disintegration in our communities.

The question for Isaac is: *Will* he dig the wells which will restore his family to their rightful familial status? *Can* he dig those wells which symbolize God's promises for the future?

The question for us today is: *Will we*, the people of God, dig or not dig the wells of hope, deliverance, liberation, and transformation for our people? *Can we* dig the wells which will *restore* confidence in ourselves and God, *empower* us to take back and rebuild our communities, and *inspire* us to have faith and courage to stand toe to toe with those oppositional forces which threaten to vanquish and annihilate us?

To paraphrase the words of that great black writer, William Shakespeare, "To dig or not to dig, that is the question."

The scriptures tell us that the land was full of famine, drought, and desolation. Abraham died and left his legacy of faith to his son Isaac. You will remember that Abraham is the Father of Our Faith because he stepped out of nowhere into a somewhere, which would become a solid watering ground for the people of God. Abraham was distinguished by his faith and obedience to God. But after venturing out into the new land, his family began experiencing the trials and tribulations of a Bedouin people. Trouble stalked them. Hardship assailed them, and they wondered if God had abandoned them in their quest for human wholeness and spiritual restoration.

As Abraham lay on his deathbed, he got Isaac's assurance that he would carry on this great legacy by trusting God and holding on to God's unchanging hand.

Isaac went to King Abimelech of the Philistines, who were some of the most powerful people on earth. People feared them, for their armies marched by day and night and vanquished enemies with terrible, lightning swiftness. They were big, smart, cunning, and daring, and known as the mighty giants who struck fear, terror, and sickness unto death in God's people. Goliath would later be known as their most notorious assailant.

God told Isaac to remain in Gerar so that he could be blessed and multiply his wealth. Isaac loved the Lord so much that he would do anything God asked of him. His trust was that deep; his faith abiding; his judgment and wisdom tempered with exacting insight.

Isaac did what he was told by God, but when approached about his wife (she must have been a fine sister), he lied about her and said she was his sibling. He did the same thing his father did before him. He was later reprimanded by Abimelech and placed in protective custody. Abimelech wanted no harm to come to Isaac and his family.

Now Isaac was a great man in his own right. He made something out of nothing by taking his talents and gifts and using them for the glory of God and the benefit of his people. He took a small parcel of land and made a vast fortune. The scriptures say he planted a crop and reaped one hundredfold. You don't need much. Just use what you've got and God can make you a prosperous person.

You see, you can use what God has given you, like Isaac, and turn it one hundredfold so that our people and communities might be strengthened and empowered. This means that everything from our dollars to our spiritual resources should be used to enhance our communities.

Isaac did so well that the Philistines became jealous of his success. He became wealthy, with hordes of servants and live-stock, and the Philistines envied him. The king said, "Isaac, you've got to get out of town. Get your things and get outta here, man, for you have become too powerful! My men are getting jealous and envious because they believe you have more than they have! They have hatred in their hearts and many of them are breathing death threats against you and have vowed to put a contract out on your life! You must leave, man, to save your own life. I would help you, brother, but my hands are tied!"

Isaac packed his things, gathered his family and community and moved to the valley of Gerar, the lowlands known for their treacherous terrain and barren and arid soil. And there he began to redig the wells his father Abraham had erected as watering places for the people of God.

After Abraham left the land, the Philistines had covered the wells with dirt as an expression of contempt for Abraham and his family. Isaac now found himself in the same valley, faced with the same enemies, and trying to decide if he would reopen the wells the enemies of his father had closed. The Philistines had already harassed him for doing so well with his little parcel of land. Now was the time to reassert himself by reaffirming the faith of his father and the confidence of God.

Isaac knew that the wells were vitally important to the life of his people. They could not live in the hot desert without water. But more importantly, the wells had far deeper meaning and value, for reopening them would symbolically tie them back to the faith of Abraham and give them new hope for the future as they faced great odds and forged a realizable future.

The wells not only hold water which is necessary for survival, but also are symbols of spiritual renewal and vitality and dogged determination to succeed against strong opposition. By redigging the wells, Isaac provides his people with not only the waters of life to sustain their lives physically, but also the waters of truth which would help sustain their lives spiritually.

By reopening the wells, Isaac seeks to recover the deep, still waters of a great family history which was displaced by Abraham's death and his people's movement to another land. By choosing to redig, he is claiming personal identity and reaffirming the power, purposes, and promises of God. So the wells have literal and figurative importance.

Your wells today might be any efforts you execute which help heal the hurt of family displacement or restore confidence in God. It might be some act, some consistent effort which seeks to unearth truth, love, justice, personal empowerment, and spiritual transformation for the people of God. The question today is: *Can You Dig It?* Can you dig these wells of love and truth in the face of major obstacles? That may be the question we face today, the United Methodist Church faces, the Christian faith faces, but certainly it is the question confronting the African-American community! We must find the resolve to keep on digging! *Can You Dig It!*

As soon as people got wind of Isaac's plans they began to sabotage the process: First, he dug the well in the valley of Gerar which became full of fresh clean water. The herdsmen of Gerar became so infuriated that they quarreled with Isaac's herdsmen over the water, but *Isaac kept on digging! Can You Dig It?*

The opposition became so strong that he named the well *Esek,* which means *strife* and *tribulation*. **The first well was thus dug for familial reclamation.** He dug the well to reclaim his family heritage, and immediately strife and tribulation followed. Familial reclamation means reaffirming, rediscovering something of supreme spiritual value of the past which will preserve our families and our communities for the future. The family is the stronghold of spiritual prosperity. There are many family values that have been forsaken, because we have too often forgotten the paths paved for us by our forebears.

68

In the case of Isaac, the well was dug to reclaim the faith of his father as a means of holding together his family. Every family has something of ultimate value which is its positive strength, its rallying juncture for helping the family preserve itself. The survival and restoration of the African-American community has depended upon teaching some spiritual value which has held the family together against the opposition and strife of slavery and other social calamities. We need to look into our personal family histories and reclaim that particular value. *Can you dig it today? The well of familial reclamation?*

African-Americans have something of positive value in their personal family histories which can become the watering ground for the revitalization of our communities.

It may be something as simple as grandma's hum or as complex as holding onto some practice or belief which sustains the family through difficult times. Some traditional and ritual practices we should unearth and preserve. Some practices of abuse we should relinquish. Every family has something of value from its past which can help it find its future.

Isaac understood the value in doing such. He was reclaiming the faith of his father as a means of living out the promises of the future. *Can You Dig It? The well of familial reclamation?*

Secondly, after continued harassment Isaac was compelled to move to a second place and dig the well **symbolizing self-determination and self-empowerment**. His enemies thought he would stop digging after the first well, but even as all hell broke loose upon him, he was determined to dig on! *Can you dig it?*

Anytime you seek to determine for yourself, define for yourself, analyze for yourself, or judge for yourself the direction your life should go, you are practicing self-determination, for as long as you have the power to define and refine reality for yourself, you can determine for yourself the purpose and direction of your life. Isaac was determined to dig the second well despite the opposition; despite strife, hatred, tribulation, and deprecation which stood in his way. He could have easily allowed fate to direct his course, but he was determined to press on.

The second well he named *Sitnah*, which means *strife* and *hatred*. We as a people, in restoring the life and sanctities of our families and our communities, must **take back the power to define for ourselves the direction of our lives** despite what others do to stop us!

One reason why so much strife infests our communities is because we are too gullible, too open and vulnerable to other folks' opinions and solutions about how to keep our own families together and how to solve our own problems. We have abandoned our own spiritual, familial, and cultural traditions for the sake of identifying with other folks, when we need to look to ourselves for solutions to our own problems. We can't determine reality and our future if we can't *define* what's real and what isn't real! We can't be free until our minds, hearts, and souls are unshackled from the inability to define who we are and why we are. We must have the freedom to analyze, define, and describe the nature of the problems which face us. We must possess the courage to press on in hope as we build a realizable future for ourselves and the larger humanity.

One couple came to me for counseling. They had been having marital problems and a previous therapist told them that they both had *personality disorders*! In looking at their situation, we discovered the problems had nothing to do with personality. *Strike one*: They were both working professionals who saw each other at the worst time of their day. *Strike two*: She was an accountant and he a lawyer. He talked all day at work. She talked to nobody. When he came home, he didn't want to talk, and she did. *Strike three*: They were both only children used to having their way. All these vocational and structural problems had to do with routine, lifestyle, and expectations. They had nothing to do with personality disorders. They had to define for themselves the real problem. This means they had to think for themselves!

We must develop power to define our own problems and develop solutions — *self-determination*! Some folks don't want you to determine for self, because it's too much power, for once you analyze your problem, you can resolve your problem — that's self-determination. *Can You Dig It? Can you dig the well of self-*

reliance and empowerment? Can you dig the wells of *independent analysis?* Can you develop your *cognitive processes* into *transcendent judgment that allows you to rise on the wings of God to see your problems from on high?*

Isaac was determined to influence his future. We as the people of God should be determined in saving and reclaiming our communities. *Can You Dig It!*

Despite Isaac's resolve, problems got so bad he moved on to the third well at *Rehoboh,* which means *this spacious place.* **Here the third well was dug for community preservation.** For it is not enough for a people in rebuilding their lives to reclaim familial values and affirm self-identity and self-determination, they must direct their energies to translate these very ideals and principles into preserving the life, integrity, and sanctity of their communities.

The Philistines understood that once Isaac and his people reclaimed their family heritage and revowed self-identity and determination they would naturally develop the resources to rebuild and empower their people to live out the claims of their faith for the future. It was here that opposition to Isaac fell off, not because his enemies got tired, but because each well dug represented a resurgence of familial and communal restoration and values which could not be hindered in the long run. Because of Isaac's perseverance in redigging the wells, he discomfited and exhausted the opposition of his enemies.

We as a people must redig the wells of familial reclamation, self-determination, and communal preservation in rebuilding the black family and its future.

Finally, Isaac moved on to Beersheba and dug the fourth well, which was for full **spiritual restoration.** The trials of digging the wells made his people stronger and their full spiritual restoration was achieved by digging the previous three wells. By reclaiming a value of our personal histories, by reasserting self-determination, and by preserving our communities, we come into full spiritual restoration. Such is the crowning achievement of our persistent labors against great opposition.

Can you dig these wells today? Can you create something of lasting value which will sustain our people and provide them with the watering places of hope and truth for the future? The Black church is still the hope of our future; the place where people will look for hope and promises of a better tomorrow. The Black family can preserve itself, love itself, nurture itself by digging those wells. Let's move on in the spirit of Isaac and keep on digging. Keep on trusting and keep on praying in His Holy Name. Don't allow the opposition to prevent you from pressing on in the revitalization of your families, your communities and your people. Keep on digging the wells of familial reclamation, self-determination and empowerment, community preservation, and spiritual restoration.

Because of Isaac's persistence and determination, his enemies decided to make peace with him out of respect for his faith.

Can You Dig It?

Shake
It Off!

Matthew 10:1-11; Acts 28:1-10

Adrenaline pulsed through our bodies as we nervously took our positions in the field. It was an important playoff game, and everyone was feeling the pressure. The second baseman dropped a routine fly in the bottom of the seventh, allowing three runs to score which tied the game. In the third inning the right fielder had uncharacteristically overrun a pop-up after losing it in the sun, permitting the first run.

Now it was the bottom of the eight inning, the score tied, runners on first and third with two outs. Their cleanup hitter was standing at the plate, windmilling that big 36-ounce stick in the pitcher's face with the look of vengeance in his eyes. Somehow I sensed he would be coming my way as I stooped down and took my defensive position. The windup. The pitch. "Pow!" The ball exploded off the bat like a Scud missile. Seeing it soar towards left-center field, I took off running to chase it down. "I got it," I shouted. "I got it," said the left fielder. "I got it," I screamed louder. "No, I got it," he said more forcefully.

"I got it! I got it! I got it!" I boomed, waving him off. "No," he said, as the ball slammed into my mitt and we collided head-on like two trains.

Stars flashing and birds singing were all I remembered as the ball rolled out of my glove. Dazed, but raising myself up from the ground like a wounded doe shot down, I spun a lazy circle, looking for the ball, hoisted it and threw it to the cutoff man as the two go-ahead runs scored.

That critical error cost us the game and knocked us out of the playoffs. A brilliant season ended with a few costly mistakes. We choked. Plain and simple. We choked! For days and weeks I was depressed, but the words of my coach kept coming back to me after the error. "Shake it off. Shake it off, son. Winners never quit and quitters never win." I'll never forget those words, and while I had been lost in a blue funk, purple haze of sadness for weeks thereafter, his consoling words kept coming back to me. "You have to shake this off, Stewart, not only physically, but emotionally. Shake it off and keep on going. Don't look back. There's always next season."

Many times since have I thought about the importance of we humans learning to shake off past mistakes and errors in the playing fields of human experience and the seasons of life itself. We must not only shake off the physical effects of our trials by fire, but also the emotional, psychological, and spiritual pain, the memory of what happened to us, in order to get on with our lives. Sometimes we have a hard time shaking things off. The memory of the experience is too stark. Still waters run deep, and the disbelief and sorrow which result from our encounters with life often hold us hostage, suspend us eternally between the memories of what happened and the possibilities of what could or should have happened.

How often we become emotionally, psychologically, and spiritually stuck because we cannot forget or forgive ourselves or others. We can't shed the excess baggage or move beyond our broken fields of dreams because the loss is too deep, the pain too piercing, the memories too vivid, the disappointment and sorrow too lingering. Somehow we just can't shake it off, let it go, close the book on the case and be done with what's been done. So we wallow and saunter and hang our heads like center fielders giving up unearned runs in championship games, never thinking there is tomorrow and that God gives us second chances.

The experience of Paul is helpful here. Here is a man who had selflessly placed himself on the altar of Christ, making the supreme sacrifice of traveling thousands of miles to spread the Good News of Christ. He is dynamic, creative, full of energy, and surely loves the Lord. He is without family. No children. He had given up all the trappings and amenities of a normal life to tell the story and preach the Word of the risen Christ.

Our scripture today finds him safely on the island of Malta, sixty miles south of Sicily, after going through storms and being shipwrecked. His troubles and trials are many. The persecution of his efforts has dramatically escalated, as he is tossed to and fro on the high seas of life like a ship without sails. We see him on the island, gathering around a fire, reaching to place a piece of brushwood in the flames. Suddenly a snake crawls out of the fire and fastens itself on his hand and he shakes it off without harm. Paul is not only unhurt but goes on to heal the father of Polonius, who had been suffering from fever and dysentery.

The experience of Paul is instructive for us, for we too must learn to shake off the serpents which have fastened themselves on us and threaten us harm. We must shake them off and go on with our lives and the Lord's work. The image of the serpent is important here because it is quiet and cunning, deadly and dangerous. They fasten on our minds and spirits, and threaten to drain the last vestiges of life from us. This serpent for Paul was a real live reptile, but more importantly becomes a symbol of those amphibious spiritual realities which keep creeping back into the foreground of our minds, experiences which threaten to destroy our confidence in God and stifle our spiritual progress. We must shake off these serpents and demons if we expect the full benefit of God's blessings as we do ministry!

This serpent that latched on Paul at this critical time of his journey represents terror, fear, doubt, sadness, depression, unforgiveness, distrust, disobedience, calamity, strife, and apathy. As Paul shook these things off, we must shake them off. The serpent threatened to harm him, thus thwarting his service and movement for God.

As believers we must shake off the memory and pain of our own past sin by confession and repentance. Life is a trial and error process. Writing seen on a biker's motorcycle jacket describes our human condition: "Born to sin." Adam passed this condition on to us. Mistakes are the experiences which teach us life's deepest lessons. In taking inventory of how we've come to learn what we know, most of our knowledge comes from errors we've made along life's way, from the sins of omission and commission. We commit sin knowingly or unknowingly. We make mistakes the same way. We must learn to put our past in perspective and understand that we cannot get through this life without such experiences.

Confession and repentance are good ways to shake off the memories of past sin and error. Confession and repentance are God's medicines to begin the healing, curing process.

We can never go back to undo what's been done, to correct our errors. But we can confess and repent, which helps us to shake off and get over the sins of our past.

The serpent fastening itself to Paul's hand might have been the memory of his past, of how he persecuted Christians and instigated the death of Stephen. After doing his great work, this serpent of past sin may have been making its way back into the forefront of his mind, causing consternation, dismay, and disbelief. He had to shake the serpent off. But he had already done this by confession and repentance.

Even after we have made our confession and repentance, we must be on guard for those adversarial forces which creep back, threatening to destroy our forward movement in life. We've all done things that we regret, but we must work hard to see that the memory of the sin or the sin itself does not slither back to fasten on us and hold us back.

One way of shaking off the pain of that dropped pop-up was by confessing my error and working hard to make sure the same mistake didn't happen again. Repentance means turning around, changing directions, and starting all over with a clean slate. God wants this for us and has made a way through Christ to make this happen. We must shake it off by confession and repentance, and forgive ourselves.

While I was a student in England, on my short breaks I would go to London and frequent Hyde Park. There was a "speakers corner" where various people from all walks of life would mount the rickety wooden platform and launch into sublime and blissful orations. From college professors to winos, sneak thieves and pickpockets, they all gathered to showcase their rhetorical wares and test their powers of human persuasion.

I recall a man named Nigel, who stumbled upon the box one gray day in the fall of 1971. In a long, black overcoat, sipping wistfully from a bottle of Harvey's Bristol Cream, he charged into one of the most magnificent Shakespearean elocutions I've ever heard! As my friend, Chris Barnet, and I sat there spellbound, Nigel then lapsed into a teary tirade of how he had killed a seven-year-old girl while driving drunk in the streets of London's East End. His pain was so deep that he fell to his knees, wailing like a wounded animal.

I shall never forget this as long as I live. The pain, the memory of that dreadful deed still haunted his waking hours like the ghosts of Hamlet. While he confessed, he could not forgive himself as God had and he drank his life away unrepentantly. Alcohol became his refuge for that painful experience.

Then there is the story of the great Gardner Taylor, prince of preachers, and Pastor Emeritus of Concord Baptist Church in Brooklyn, New York, who knew of a person who was killed by another person while driving his car. The pain of that memory never left him, but the man confessed, repented, and forgave himself. He turned his life around and became a preacher, much like Paul, and never looked back. Ironically, Taylor's wife was later killed by a motorist.

We must learn to shake off the devastation of our past misdeeds and our past mistakes, confess our sin, ask for forgiveness, and repent by turning our lives around for the better. God has not given up on you. Why should you give up on yourself? We can redress our misdeeds by doing good things.

Second, **we must learn to shake off the memory and pain of others' past sin against us by exercising forgiveness through prayer and petition.**

It is true that forgiveness must be preceded by repentance. It's hard sometimes to forgive when the transgressor has no repentant attitude. But we must still find ways of shaking the whole thing off. Too many of us are still stuck on what someone else did to us too long ago.

A classic case of forgiveness is Jacob and Esau. Jacob did not think that his brother would forgive him after all those years after stealing his birthright, but Jacob was surprised that Esau had forgiven him.

One of the greatest deterrents to our spiritual progress is our inability to shake off the things done to us by others. We can't get on with our lives because we are still angry and hurt by another's sin against us. We must find ways of redirecting our antagonism into something higher. We must channel our hurt, our anger, our despair, and our disappointment into something positive. Let go. Unpack the baggage. Stop wallowing in the quagmires of the past. Get your passport stamped and move on to higher ground, to your next destination.

Jesus exhorts his disciples in Matthew 10. If the people do not receive you, don't get stuck. Don't waste your life away crying crocodile tears; "shake" the dust from your feet and keep on moving. Don't get put in spiritual, emotional, and psychological jail by the things other people do to you. After it's done, don't give them the keys to your jail cell by living in solitary confinements of unhappiness and pain. Get out of jail, pass go, and collect two hundred!

Jesus provides a classic example of how to use negative energy by turning it into something constructive. In Mark 3:5, he is confronted by the Pharisees for healing. The scriptures say that he looked at them with anger, then told the man to stretch out his hand and be healed! He took the harm of others and turned his anger into healing for someone else.

Remember that classic scene in the movie *Gandhi*, where a Muslim man comes to the Mahatma, confessing his murder of a Hindu boy's father? "What shall I do?" asks the man. "Raise the boy as your own, but raise him as a Hindu," Gandhi says. Take what you have done and channel it into something good. Don't dwell on what you did or what was done to you. Shake it off!

Paul again, after shaking off the serpent, heals the father of Polonius. The people were waiting for Paul to drop dead, to manifest the residue of the viper's bite. But he shook it off and channeled the energy into helping someone else. Shake it off.

What's wrong? Are you still carrying the memory of the painful things that have happened to you? Shake it off. Are you still wallowing in self-pity, anger, doubt, disillusionment, betrayal, heartbreak, and heartache? Shake it off! Are you stuck on going nowhere road? Have you lost your job? Have you lost your girl-friend or boyfriend? They didn't treat you right or give you what you thought you deserved after you worked so hard to please that person? Shake it off! Whether you've been pink-slipped or dung-dipped, shake it off. God wants you to move on and get a life! Don't ever let others' sins against you stop you from making progress and getting on with your life! Pray about it! Ask God to relieve you of the burdens of the pain. Ask God to unbind you, to release you from the brunt of the hurt. Pray constantly to be let go of the painful memory of what's happened to you. Take that anger, that hurt, that frustration, and channel it into some good work for God.

What did Robert Monroe do after being wrongfully accused of murder and rape after spending twenty years in jail? He shook it off by finishing high school and going to college. He's now graduated and running a successful business! He didn't get stuck on what unjustly happened to him. He shook it off and got on with his life! When asked the key to his positive outlook his response was one word, "PRAYER!"

What did James Earl Jones do after being teased so badly by his fellow schoolmates for stuttering so terribly that he could barely utter an audible word? He shook it off and is now one of the most articulate and successful actors in Hollywood!

What did Marian Anderson do when told by the Daughters of the American Revolution that she couldn't sing in Constitution Hall because of her race? She shook it off and sang before thousands at the Lincoln Memorial with the help of the great Eleanor Roosevelt!

What did Kathy Bates do when she was told that she was too fat and unattractive to be a leading lady in Hollywood? She shook it off by winning an Oscar for her role in the movie *Misery*!

As a superstar on the gridiron, O.J. Simpson learned early on the meaning of shaking off the hard licks and tough kicks. Now, faced with the greatest battle of his life, he's got to shake it off and keep on running for the prize, which is now his own life!

What did Jesus do after the Good Friday execution? He shook it off Easter morning by getting up from the grave!

What did I do after dropping that fly ball and ending our season? The next year we won the playoffs, and I didn't drop a fly ball the whole year. No errors. I shook it off so tough they called me the human vacuum cleaner. Anything that looked like it was flying in the vicinity of center field got sucked into my glove. I climbed fences. I jumped walls. I slid on grass with shoestring catches. I left no stone unturned and no avenue unexplored and if the right or left fielder didn't hear me when I said, "I got it," baseball would turn into football and somebody would pay hard and it wouldn't be me. I shook it off. I prayed. I asked God for forgiveness and I forgave myself. In the third game of the playoffs, we collided again but with different results.

We as God's people must shake off the bad things we've done through confession and repentance and shake off the bad things done to us through prayer and forgiveness and press on towards the mark!

Shake off sin, doubt, disappointment, and the pain of disillusionment and despair. Stand up this morning and shake it off. Whatever your problem, tell yourself to shake it off. Get a life and move on from the things which are holding you back!

Living Beyond
Unhappily Ever After

Genesis 21:8-12; Luke 7:11-17; 21:1-4

The story escalated towards its climax as viewers sat breathlessly riveted to their seats. The beautiful young woman stands in the doorway, tears cascading down her cheeks as she pans the green rolling hills of her 100-acre estate, looking for Joel. The camera follows her eyes, peering towards the large iron gate fronting her palatial abode. Then suddenly appearing is the faint figure of a dashing young man, clad in resplendent blue military decor, red scarf flowing in the wind, with high black saddle boots, sterling silver sword at his side, galloping gallantly on a white horse toward the house. "He has come back for me!" she sobs, "Thank God, he has come back for me," she sighs, pulling up the hems of her big dress and running onto the winding road to meet her shining hero. Their eyes meet in a halo of passion as he dismounts, embraces her in his arms, and salutes her with a long, searing kiss as the camera fades to black. The End.

This story, as with so many Hollywood movies, ends happily ever after. Her lost love has come back for her. Her greatest dreams have come true and she will live the rest of her life under the blissful canopy of eternal tranquility. Her story ends happily ever after, but many stories in real life do not.

From the day we are born, we are fed a steady dose of happily-ever-after tales, where knights in shining armor come back from the battlefields of war to win back their virtuous and patient lovers, where the oppressed break free from the chains of servitude, and the victims of justice have their triumphant day in court. The story ends with love requited and justice retributed, for as one Hollywood director stated, "It's all about how the story ends." The

81

consumer must be satisfied with the ending for the movie to have lasting value and satisfaction.

Whether it's Curious George, Charlie Brown, Snoopy, or Dr. Seuss, the ending must blend with the harmony of the movie's musical score. *Beauty and the Beast, Aladdin* and *Dumbo* all end with the protagonists winning out over their adversaries. This is the stuff of fairy tales. This is the stuff of our happily ever afters.

But as we grow into adulthood, and the veils of innocence and ignorance are stripped from us, we come painfully to understand that every life episode does not have a storybook or Hollywood ending. Even Humpty Dumpty couldn't be put back together again by all the king's horses and all the king's men. We adults must live with the reality that every story does not end with lovers holding hands, or warriors coming back from war for their lovers unscathed and unmaimed, or the pendulums of justice swinging unhampered in the balances for the oppressed. We adults must learn to live beyond our unhappily-ever-after experiences. This is the true test of both our character and our spirituality.

While our three scripture lessons spotlight the lives of three women whose endings were not happily ever after, they are relevant to men, women, boys, and girls who have struggled in the quagmires of disappointment, despair, and unhappy epilogues.

In the first instance we have Hagar in Genesis 21. Here is a woman who loved Abraham dearly. There is no doubt that she was in love with the man, but Abraham, at the jealous and envious entreaties of his wife Sarah, puts Hagar and her son Ishmael out to die on the desert. What did she do to deserve this? The scriptures say that Sarah was upset that Ishmael mocked her son Isaac and asked that Hagar not receive Abraham's inheritance. Abraham was hurt by this prospect, but cautioned by God that it would be the right thing to do. God would give an inheritance to both Isaac and Ishmael. Abraham felt a little better about this, but it did not allay the grief he felt in having to put his maidservant and child out.

Putting Hagar and the child out on the desert for certain death would be a story with an unhappy ending for Hagar. Why would he do such a thing to her? Why the desert? The loneliest, most desolate place on earth? Her heart was truly broken by this inexplicable act. She loved the man. She needed the man. She had a child for the man, for it was Sarah who originally suggested that Hagar bear children for her and Abraham since Sarah was barren. It was Sarah's suggestion that Hagar be taken in and Sarah's suggestion that Hagar be put out to die.

What an unhappy situation! Hagar, while on the desert, knowing both she and her son would soon perish, heard her son cry out in thirst, but an angel of the Lord comforted her and told her where to find water on the desert. Ishmael later grew up and became an archer in the desert. Some say he is the true father of the Islamic people and their faith, but what about Hagar? There is no mention of her. She found a wife for her son from Egypt, but what about her? Did she die from heartbreak? Her story does not end happily, for once she was Abraham's mainstay and now she was an outcast from his love, a refugee from his disaffection.

Some people might say that Hagar's story did end happily ever after because instead of dying on the desert she found water and survived. But the truth is this one experience was so devastating to her that it might have overshadowed her conquest of the desert. That one heartbreak may have become the defining litany for her entire life. Yes, she survived, but it was a bittersweet memory. She might have thought herself better off dead.

How many stories have ended this way? You start out on the good foot and end up walking hot coals barefooted. You start out on Lovers' Lane and end up in Heartbreak Hotel. An episode of your life begins with all the promise of success and fulfillment and then suddenly your dreams have been dashed and your aspirations crash to earth like falling meteors. The truth is your shining moments are your life-defining moments and when the shine loses its luster, when, after the honeymoon, the honey comes off the moon, when so much of who you are is based upon how happy you are, and when you experience unhappiness, your life falls apart. When things don't go according to plan, we human beings tend to come apart at the seams and live the rest of our lives unhappily, in despair and without the spiritual capacity to overcome what's happened to us. In fact, the thing that happens to us makes us virtually unhappy for the rest of our lives. That one episode becomes the defining element of all our remaining experiences. Jilted lovers can sometimes never love again because that one tragedy has made them so bitter that they can't start over. One writer said, **"Success is getting what you want and happiness is wanting what you get."**

We don't know about Hagar, but we know about those countless millions who can't get beyond the one heartbreak, the one calamity, the one persecution, the one central, overarching, defining life experience that colors all their future expectations and aspirations. They cannot get beyond that one unhappily-ever-after experience that brought them so low they never will rise again.

But the fact that Hagar found water in the desert is a metaphor for those who can't get beyond that one unhappy experience. There are other watering places, other possibilities even in the most unlikely and impossible situations. There is life beyond divorce court, life beyond broken dreams and discomfited plans. There is life beyond the battlefields, the cold wars, and the long fights. Life even beyond the broken dreams of the cemetery.

Keep looking for the watering places. Don't give up your search. Although one experience may have ended unhappily, it doesn't have to be the single defining encounter in your life, shaping your response to all future possibilities. We must remember that our life stories are much, much more than that one tragic act; the one grim interlude; that one painful episode. There is so much more to our lives than the painful experiences we encounter. But we must all work hard never to let the things which happen to us in the story dictate the ending.

Our second scripture in Luke 7:11-17 finds the widow who is unhappy because she has lost both her husband and son.

The death of her loved ones has cast a specter of unhappiness over her life. Death can do this. When someone close to you dies, someone you love and cherish, you feel you have been robbed of a most precious gift. This death is the one death that shapes your perspective on the rest of your days and you live forever unhappy. Death causes unhappiness because of our relationships, our loves, our attachments, and our memories of those deceased.

We ask God why this person has been taken from us. We question God through the process. And the rest of our days become one dark liturgy of despair and sorrow because death has both instigated our misery and invaded our premises like unwanted bill collectors.

But the widow, faced with a double indemnity, manages to overcome her hurt for a short enough time to seek Jesus. The story goes that Jesus touched the coffin of her dead son and he rose again.

We might look at this passage from two different vantage points, spiritual death and physical death. The physically dead are buried in coffins made of wood and cast-iron steel. The spiritually dead are existing within coffins of despair, fear, self-doubt, affliction, spiritual pestilence, lechery, ignorance, and the vicious cycles of disaffection and self-destruction. Our story does not have to end unhappily when someone we love physically dies because Jesus can touch them in death, and those who die in him are with him now, have life now, have power now, have joy now, have solace, peace, and eternal happiness now! Although you cannot experience their physical presence, you know they are with Christ, that they are alive and well, and that if you die in Christ you will see them again when you get to the other side!

But there are those who have lost people close to them through spiritual death. There are many spiritually dead. You have tried every means to reach them, to revive them, to bring them back to spiritual life, and to put them on the right course with God. Their coffins might be coffins of shame, sorrow, disappointment, affliction, and other maladies that keep them from full spiritual happiness. Spending their days among the tombs, they have nothing for which to live.

A woman confessed one day that her unhappiness is because her son is a bum. He doesn't work. He won't look for work and he always wears B.U.M. t-shirts. He has all the opportunities in the world to succeed but he won't, and his life is caught in the spin cycle of drug and alcohol abuse. I said to her one day, "Your story with your son doesn't have to end unhappily, because Jesus is still the man with the plan. Jesus can change lives and bring back to life the spiritually dead. I've seen him touch the coffins of alienation and make estranged people lovers again. I've seen him touch the coffins of disappointment, despair, trouble, sorrow, sickness, persecution, and every malady known to man and woman, and restore spiritual wholeness. Jesus has the power to touch the souls of the living dead and bring them back full circle. Don't live your life unhappily because one person, one situation, one circumstance, or one condition is bringing you down. Pray for a miracle, tarry in God's word, sincerely ask God to touch, like the widow did, and he can and will turn it all around. And if this doesn't happen according to plan, you make sure you keep touch with Christ, because even if other stories don't end happily in your life, your main story which is your relationship with God does."

The widow kept seeking Christ despite these two unhappy interludes in her life. And this brings us to an important point: You cannot break off your relationship with God and expect to be blissfully happy. Robert Frost has a great poem which contains a line reading, *"I had a lover's quarrel with the world."* Well, some of us have a lover's quarrel with God. Because we've had experiences which end unhappily, we turn away from the main source of our eternal joy, Christ. Some of us, because of an unhappy ending, will give up on God, will cut God off without realizing that it is our relationship with God that helps us overcome the unhappy episodes of our lives. It's a viable relationship with Christ that helps us catapult the maladies and the tragedies of our human experiences. It's our relationship with God which becomes the window through which we interpret the remaining sagas of our lives. Not the widow! She kept seeking Christ, because she knew that the right relationship with Christ would help her overcome her grief, sorrow, and disappointment at the deaths of her husband and son.

The point here is that while episodes or experiences in our lives may end unhappily, our relationship with Christ never does. For it is our relationship with God that shapes our attitudes and responses to our life experiences. If we have a verified, bona fide relationship with Jesus, we can surmount the unhappily-ever-after syndromes which force us into the spiritual doldrums. If our relationship with God becomes the central underlying influence on how we look at our experiences and how we respond to them, our lives can never have an unhappy ending. While we may have episodes that end unhappily, our whole lives do not have to be a tale told by an idiot full of sound and fury, signifying nothing. If we have Christ in our lives, we may experience unhappiness without our entire lives becoming a three-part tragedy.

We don't know if Hagar lived happily beyond her unhappily ever after, but we know that the widow did by seeking the touch of Christ. You can live beyond your unhappily ever afters by seeking Christ in all things — by seeking his grace, his touch and his mercy, by immersing yourself in his word and his work, by developing a disciplined devotional life and by being obedient to his will for your life. There is nothing like working for and through Christ. Whatever your sorrow or challenge today, you don't have to live unhappily ever after because God has a way of making things better for those who truly seek God and work faithfully for God.

Finally, we find in our Luke 21 text another widow who goes to the treasury to put something into the church. Could this be the same widow who lost her son some passages earlier? Without the risk of isogesis, let's speculate that it's the same woman, who didn't have very much but is coming to the synagogue to put something into the church. The point here is that if it's the same widow, she is living beyond her poverty, beyond her heartbreak and heartache by giving back to God something of worth and value. She does not let her unhappiness brought on by her poverty of purse stop her from giving back to God. In other words, her poverty of purse does not create within her a poverty of mind and spirit. If it's the same woman, she not only lived beyond her unhappily ever after by seeking the touch of Jesus, she now is giving something back to the church even when she has no means for doing so. She is living beyond her unhappiness by going where she would dare not go, giving what she cannot give and trusting in God enough to make a worthy sacrifice.

Jesus was pleased with this widow because she did not allow the death of her husband to become a stumbling block to her joy, which is giving to God. The key to joy and happiness is giving to God. This is the formula for spiritual success. Perhaps our misery, our unhappiness, our pain, our sorrow, our confusion, our trouble, our malady, our trepidation, our alienation, our oppression, our depression, and our repression are directly proportionate to our refusal to give what God requires of us.

As human beings we must find ways of living beyond our unhappy endings. As Christians we believe that faith in Christ, trust in Christ, and love of Christ will help us live beyond our fields of broken dreams.

I know a man who can help you beyond your one-step beyond; a man who, at the touch of his hand, the whisper of his voice, can set you free and make you whole again. All the king's horses and all the king's men might not put Humpty together again, but I know a man who will, if you fall off the wall, pick you up and put you back together again. All we have to do is to learn how to touch him, give to him, seek him in all things, and we can get beyond the beyond that keeps us from getting on with our lives.

Accept what has happened to you in your life and know that it does not have to be the defining moment around which the rest of your life is suspended. Don't let unrequited love, as with Hagar, death or disappointment, as with the widows, stop you from living happily. Get on with your life. Get a life and move on in Christ.

Know that it's your response to situations that determines how well you adjust and live beyond your hurts.

Keep seeking and trusting Christ in all things.

Prayer, devotion, Bible study, and actively seeking God will be the means of overcoming the sorrow, pain, and troubles of this life.

We can live beyond unrequited love, as with Hagar, and the death of our loved ones, as with the widow, and poverty of purse does not mean poverty of mind and spirit as with the widow's mite. Trusting Christ means that while some episodes in our lives may have ended unhappily, our life in Christ always ends so happily!

Let It Shine!

John 1:1-14

The Gospel of John makes one of the most powerful observations in all scripture: "In the beginning was The Word, and the Word was with God and the Word was God. The same was in the beginning with God. All things were made by him; and without him was not any thing made that was made. In him was life and that life was the light of men. And the light shineth in the darkness and the darkness comprehended it not." (KJV)

The Moffatt translation of the Bible says, "And the light shines in the darkness and the darkness has not *mastered* it."

The New International Version of the Bible says, "And the light shines in the darkness and the darkness has not *understood* it."

Perhaps the most comprehensive statement is found in the Amplified Bible, which says, "And the light shines in the darkness, for the darkness has not *overpowered* it — *put it out*, or has not *absorbed* it, has not *appropriated* it and is *unreceptive to it.*"

The Amplified Bible provides the most definitive statement of this passage, for the darkness has not overpowered the light, put it out, absorbed it, or appropriated it and is thoroughly unreceptive to it. It is this translation of John 1:5 that I wish to elaborate today. Before dealing with the meaning of the Amplified Bible's version of this passage, I want to talk about the function and purpose of darkness and light in two principal realms: the physical realm at the beginning of creation and the spiritual realm at the beginning of the second creation with the coming of Christ.

In Genesis we find discussion of darkness in the physical realm. Genesis 1:2 says that the earth was formless and empty, darkness was over the surface of the deep, and the Spirit of God was hovering over the waters. Then God said, "Let there be light."

91

Before light was created by God, darkness had already been created as a first principle. The darkness was already in existence before God called the light into being. Many people say that God created light first with the words, "Let there be light," but if God created everything and the darkness existed prior to God's calling the light into existence, this means that God had to have created the darkness first. First, the darkness was created and then God called light into being.

Let me say that the original function of darkness was to serve as a help structure, a supporting cast for the light. The original purpose of darkness was to help the light be seen; to help the light stand out; to help the light reach its apex and function by providing a black backdrop to the light. We all know that the light is best seen in darkness. So when God created darkness, God created it to have a specific function and that function was to help the light irradiate in the most brilliant manner possible. The light best shines when it has a black background. The darkness was originally intended to embrace the light, surround the light, provide the light with a black canopy or canvass against which the light would greatly standout. The original purpose of physical darkness as created by God is to function in harmony with the light so that light and darkness would complement each other, work together in a collaborative manner.

It was not necessary for the darkness to say to the light, "I am better than you. I am greater than you. I am more desirable than you. God prefers me more than you." There was no reason for the darkness to try to overcome the light. No reason for the darkness to set up a conspiracy to take the light from the light because the light could only do its best work in conjunction with the darkness.

So in the beginning the darkness and light were like husband and wife; they were opposite poles of the same principle. They functioned as a closely knit unit in creation — each complementing and beautifying the other; each providing the other with the necessary support; each adoring and adorning the other with the elements to help each do its best work.

This is the function of light and darkness in the physical realm. This is what God intended in the first creation: that darkness and light become soul mates, helpmates, in the created order of creation. Each would function according to God's master plan of the universe. Each would function with its appointed tasks with equal hours in creation. Each would keep watch over certain portions of the earth in its equally allotted time slot.

But something happened that changed all that. The scriptures say that God began to set into the universe different qualities or gradations of light. Genesis 1:4 says that God said that the light was good, and separated the light from darkness. Note now that God did not say the darkness was good, but that the light was good. God called the light day and the darkness night.

We also find in Genesis 1:14 that God began further to separate the day and the night and used them to mark the seasons, days, and years, and God put lights in the sky in the form of stars. Genesis 1:16 says that God made two great lights, the *greater* light to govern the day, and the *lesser light* to govern the night. While God had created these two realities initially to coexist in harmony, we find that the conditions are set in motion to place night and day at odds with each other. Note that in Genesis 1:31 God saw all that God had made and it was very good. According to God, light and darkness were good because he created them, but somehow the darkness did not comprehend this fact of creation and the struggle of light and darkness was established in the physical realm. This struggle of light and darkness would translate into every realm of creation. Perhaps the darkness had a problem with God calling the light good and God not calling the darkness good.

Whatever the case, the terms and conditions of the war of light and darkness were set into creation.

Whereas darkness and light were originally created to function and coexist in harmony, when God began separating them and valuing them, the terms for the struggle between light and darkness began. In the beginning they were created as soul mates, but as God began to separate them, jealousy, envy, and competition set in between these entities. The darkness became envious of the light because God called it good. The darkness became envious of the light because the light would have first priority.

God said there would be day first and then night. The darkness may not have liked being put in second place, in second order, playing second fiddle. The darkness may not have liked this because it was here first. The darkness existed before God created light and now the light would be first in the form of day and darkness second in the form of night.

Whether we have a literal or figurative interpretation of the creation story, the fact is the conditions of light and darkness were established in the first creation, and that by naming the light good, and by making day a greater light and night a lesser light, the terms were set for the struggle of light and darkness in physical creation.

In the physical realm darkness and light have been forever in competition and that struggle translated into humanity, into spiritual creation, into the war of darkness and light for the souls of humankind. We find that Adam and Eve sinned not only because they disobeyed God, but also because the darkness won out over Adam's and Eve's souls. Because the competition or war of light and darkness had been set in motion in creation resulting in good and evil, Adam and Eve fell in to spiritual darkness by their sin against God. The war for men's and women's souls in the spiritual realm may have been set at creation in the Garden, resulting in Adam's and Eve's loss of light. They allowed the reality of darkness to overcome the light of God in them.

In the second creation, with the coming of Jesus, we find that God is trying to re-establish the supremacy of that light in the souls of humankind. God is not trying to re-create physical creation, but re-create and configure the souls and spirits of humankind, because there is so much darkness that the light threatens to be snuffed out, overcome. So God sent another light to the world, the light which was also present in the first creation, but now is a light shining in the souls and hearts of God's people. God sent Christ to the world so that the light could regain its power and ascendancy in the souls of God's people. These powers don't like this light but can't put it out.

And so in the spiritual realm we find in the Gospel of John that God has brought a great light in the form of Christ: a light of hope, love, joy, forgiveness, and spiritual prosperity. Those who bear witness to that light must capture that light in the sanctuary of their souls and continue to let that light shine in the darkness.

John says a light shines in the darkness and now the darkness cannot overpower it, cannot put it out, cannot absorb it, cannot appropriate it, cannot be receptive to it. This is the word to those in the new creation of Christ. The spiritual darkness is threatening to blow your light out, and as long as you have the light of Christ in your life that light can never be snuffed out.

Stop hiding your light under the bushel. Isaiah says, "Arise, shine for your light has come."

Again, let us go back to the Amplified Translation of the Bible. Many people whom God has thoroughly and tremendously blessed are still struggling with whether to shine that light. They still apologize to people for what God has given them. For too long now they have sold out their souls to the darkness. They have allowed the darkness to overcome their light. They have reduced their spiritual incandescence in order to let the darkness feel more comfortable. You have hidden your light under a bushel because the darkness has threatened to overcome your light.

The Amplified Translation says that you must remember to continue shining your light, first of all, because the darkness cannot **overpower** it. Overpower is a key word because it suggests allowing your light to be overpowered through spiritual, physical, or psychological intimidation. The people of God have been intimidated into reducing the glow of their light. The Bible says a light shines in the darkness and the darkness cannot overpower it. You may have people in your life, in your world, who have tried to instill fear in you, intimidate you into reducing your flame, but you shouldn't give them the satisfaction. All they want to do is overpower you, threaten you, and discourage you from shining your light. Let your light shine.

Look at the world. People are afraid, fearful, paranoid, suspicious, and unhappy because they have allowed the children of darkness to overpower them. People can't walk the streets anymore in darkness for fear of their lives. Spiritual darkness has so overcome and overpowered our lives that we are afraid to stand for right, for truth, for justice. We are afraid to stand for the light. We are afraid and intimidated because the darkness has overpowered us, and we are running scared for our lives.

Second, there is a light shining in the darkness and the darkness cannot **put it out**. Just as overpowering suggests spiritual, physical, and psychological intimidation to keep you from shining your light, to have your light put out is to allow the spiritual, physical, and psychological forces to annihilate your light. Not only do they want to overpower your light, but if they can they will eliminate, annihilate, and obliterate your light. They will stop at nothing to put your light completely out. That's what's wrong with some of us today. We allow the forces of envy, evil, and injustice to put our lights out completely so that we no longer have joy, no longer have confidence, assurance, and trust in God. Stop allowing the forces of evil, envy, deceit, and power to put your light out. God made you an intelligent, productive, worthwhile person and no person, no power, no principality has the right to snuff out that light, to put that light out. But if you have the light of Christ in you, it is an inextinguishable flame. It is imperishable. It cannot be put out!

Third, the darkness cannot **absorb** this light. Absorbing your light means that there are spiritual, physical, and psychological forces that will saturate your light. They can't overpower your light through intimidation. They can't put out your light through annihilation, so they try to absorb your light through saturation. These forces are a little more diplomatic and discreet. They don't use outright scare tactics like the intimidators and annihilators. They use guile and cunning, because they smile in your face and stab you in your back. They shake your hand with their finger on the trigger. They are not man nor woman enough to tell you to your face that they don't like you, so they try to absorb and saturate your light by undermining that light through clandestine means. They ingratiate themselves with you and make you feel like you're one of them so as to saturate your light. Your light already outshines them but since they couldn't intimidate or annihilate, they'll saturate you under the guise of legitimacy and goodness. Let your light shine.

Don't let the saturators steal your light. These saturators are everywhere. On the job. Maybe in your home. Even sometimes in the church. They make an art of faking left and going right. They never want you to shine and the moment you do they've got some reason to soak you up so you won't shine your light!

Fourth, the darkness cannot **appropriate** your light. Now after intimidation, annihilation, and saturation, you think folks would go somewhere and sit down and leave you alone. But there's another group. They try to appropriate your light. They use spiritual, physical, and psychological forces to legislate your light. They do it through the group process; through the committee mandate; through legal caveat. They can't intimidate you, annihilate you, or saturate you, so the next logical thing is to legislate your light right out of existence. All under the pretext of making things better for everybody.

These persons begin to use labels to devalue you as a person. Words such as *arrogant, not a team player, overqualified, militant, aloof, distant, unapproachable, upstart, egotistical.* These words are used to devalue your worth so they can legislate your light right out of existence. Their whole design is to get you to lower your opinion of yourself — make you think you're boasting because you shine the light God gave you. They want you to feel bad about being a superstar so they use machinations and gambits to make you lower your expectations and standards of yourself and others around you. They specialize in bringing out the worst in you because they have such a low opinion of themselves. Watch out for the legislators of the light. They'll vote your light right out of service.

The legislators cannot appropriate this light. Stop trying to fit in with those around you. Sometimes you have to go along to get along, but don't sell out God to the devil. Don't trade in your soul for a few glad moments of cheap grace. God has given you a light and that light is to shine at all times, especially in the darkness. Don't compromise that light to darkness. Don't let those of darkness around you, who are intimidated and envious of you, trick you into appropriating what God has given you. Let your light shine!

Fifth, since they can't intimidate, annihilate, saturate, or legislate your light out of existence, now they are totally **unreceptive** to your light. Now they outright repudiate your light. Not to accept something is to repudiate, to reject, something as completely useless. Whatever you do, those of darkness will be unreceptive to your light. There are some people who are so insecure, so self-satisfied, so envious, so jealous, so low in their self-esteem that no matter what you do, they will never be receptive to you. You can cry crocodile tears. You can go the second, third, fourth, and fifth mile to please them. You can wine them and dine them. You placate them, elevate them, and ingratiate yourself with them, and they still have a problem with you. They repudiate everything you do or ever try to do right out of existence because they really don't care about you, about how you feel, or about your well-being as a person. So now they are downright unreceptive to you.

But you keep letting your light shine. Don't turn if off. Don't put it out. Don't let the spiritual, physical, emotional, and psychological forces and powers intimidate you, annihilate you, saturate you, legislate you, or repudiate you. Because there is a light shining in the darkness and the darkness cannot overpower it, cannot put it out, cannot absorb it, cannot appropriate it, and cannot be receptive to it. So let your light shine! God gave you the light in the first place. If somebody can take it away, God can, but God doesn't want to take it. God wants you to use it!

> So if you have love, give it.
> A talent, develop it.
> A gift, share it.
> A seed, plant it.
> A harvest, reap it.
> A mind, use it.
> A test, ace it.
> Money, invest it.
> A problem, solve it.
> An obstacle, hurdle it.
> A trial, win it.
> A book, read it.

Fruit, bear it.
A hat, wear it.
A thorn, prick it.
A tree, pick it.
A task, do it.
A song, sing it.
A business, grow it.
A poem, write it.
A project, complete it.
A light, shine it!
A church, serve and support it!

Let it shine. Use what God has given you or lose what God has given you. Let your light shine for Christ. There is a light shining in the darkness and the darkness cannot overpower it, put it out, absorb it, appropriate it, or be receptive to it, so let it shine!

Just as the physical darkness got jealous when God said the light was good and separated them from each other, God has called you to be separate, apart, because you have something good. Now you need to stop trying to make those of lesser quality, lesser instinct, lesser capacity be receptive to you. God gave you more light. Shine your light. God didn't call you to compromise your gifts, talents, and skills to make the children of darkness comfortable. Let your light shine for Jesus and get a good life! Put Christ in your life, and light the eternal flame of goodness for you and those around you. Let it shine! Let it shine! Let it shine! Keep shining your light!

Paradoxes Of
The Christian Faith

Matthew 10:34-39

There is something strange and paradoxical about the faith of Christians, and many people struggle to understand how we can celebrate the life of someone who died on a cross; someone who didn't fit the conventional criteria of success; someone who brought good and joy to the world, yet was executed by the very people to whom he brought goodness. How could God take someone who was penniless and make us wealthy; someone who was homeless and provide us with a many-roomed mansion in our Father's house? What a paradox!

Many people find the central beliefs of the Christian faith very strange indeed. They do not understand how God could choose a savior *of the* world who would *die by the **hands** of the world*; and that the day of his amazing death would be Good Friday: Here was a king, born not in a palace but a pigsty, not in the big house but a kind of outhouse, one whose family was so poor they couldn't afford a room in the inn at the time of his birth. A king whose family was so indigent that when it came time for tribute at the Temple, his mother brought a turtle dove because she couldn't afford a more expensive sacrifice. He was a king from a low-income blue-collar family, born in the rundown ghetto of the backwashes of an obscure town called Bethlehem.

Our scripture exemplifies this paradox — "He who finds shall lose and he who loses shall find it."

The Christian faith is a strange and paradoxical faith. A paradox is something that seems illogical and inimical to common sense and customary experience. A paradox is something which seems contradictory to the usual, normative patterns of interpretation and understanding. It seems untrue but is true. For example, it is a paradox that America, the richest nation in the world, is the world's greatest debtor. It is a paradox that 78 percent of all professing and confessing Christians never read the Bible; a paradox that 90 percent of all Christians never have family prayer; a paradox that the United Methodist Church, which began as a Holy Ghost, Spirit-filled movement, is today not known for its spiritual fervor. It is a paradox that after all the centuries of persecution and hardship, where dictators, spectators, and agitators have heaped untold scorn on the people of God, the Christian faith is still alive and well. Anything which seems out of character or pattern with the usual flow of things is a paradox. It is quite paradoxical that women, who were the mainstays of Jesus' movement, are often spiritually taken for granted and rejected, but today there are more women in our seminaries than men!

The Christian faith seems paradoxical because God called a lowly carpenter to rule the world, to walk on water, to cast out demons, and to raise the dead. A man who, according to the historian Josephus, had his own spinal kyphosis and lived with his own spiritual and physical pain, but was called to eradicate the spiritual and physical pain of the world. He wasn't a scholar and never wrote volumes of books but has had more books written on his life by more scholars than any other person in history. He never went to medical school, but dispenses more cures in his words and touch than any hospital or infirmary in the history of humankind.

It is paradoxical that the great carpenter should be executed with the tools of his own trade: nails, hammers, and beams of wood. His birth bed and deathbed, a cradle and a cross, were made of wood. It is a paradox that the cross, which was an emblem of death, is a plus sign in Christian spirituality. The cross represents two extremities of our condition, one horizontal and the other vertical. Was this meant to be some form of mockery? How paradoxical that a man who came to heal families, husbands and wives, sons and fathers, mothers and daughters, had no wife or children of his own.

It is strange and paradoxical that the more hardship, persecution, turmoil, and suffering, the stronger some Christians get for the battle. Many people are weakened by what happens to them in life. The disappointment, heartbreak, heartache, loss, suffering, and despair finally catch up with them and knock them down to the canvas of defeat or for a standing eight count. These people have been beaten down so much they give up all hope, lose trust and confidence in God. But there are those living through each moment of possible defeat and despair who develop a stronger relationship with God. It is paradoxical that some people should be humiliated by pain and suffering while others triumph over it. Happy is the person who goes down swinging. Happier is the person who gets up swinging.

There is something strange about the Christian faith. The core truths of Christian spirituality reveal a logic which defies common sense and human nature, where negatives become positives, where crooked ways are made straight and high places low, where cornerstones rejected become the chief cornerstones, where faith the size of mustard seeds can move mountains and rock nations, where those losing their lives find them and those finding their lives lose them. That's why Jesus said, "He who has ears let him hear ... *whosoever loses his life shall find it and whosoever finds it shall lose it.*"

The Christian faith is filled with these seeming paradoxes, reverse endings, strange, logic-defying, mind-boggling, tongue-twisting, earth-shattering, heaven-heartening events which both dismay and perplex, defy and confound human understanding.

To be Christian is to embrace these seeming inconsistencies, these spiritual irregularities, these affirmations of possibilities amid disabilities and ecstasies amid tragedies.

Three central paradoxes form the foundation of Christian belief, thought, and action: **Glory out of suffering, victory out of defeat, and gain out of loss**.

The first, **glory out of suffering**, is really strange, for I can hear you saying, "Preacher, how can one obtain glory from suffering? For suffering is humiliating. It suppresses, represses, and oppresses. How can you claim 'hallelujah' glory out of 'woe is me' suffering?"

I think time and again how Christians claim it. How the great writer George Friedrich Handel claimed it in writing his *Messiah* in those 24 grueling, poverty-stricken days, when limbs were palsied and body frail. Yet in all his suffering, the spirit of Christ quickened his resolve and fueled his creative adrenaline like quicksilver on smooth surfaces. He heard the voice of Jesus and saw the heavens resound with the glory of Christ. Handel's own calamities and personal suffering would not prevent him from experiencing the glory of the Messiah. And while the music did not gain great notoriety and popularity during his day, it is nevertheless one of the greatest compositions of all time. The suffering was great but the glory magnificent! Time and again we've seen it, where the crucibles of human suffering have strengthened the people of God, where in great moments of agonizing pain and suffering they turn it in for a crown of joy. He who loses his life shall find it. He who finds it shall lose it.

Suffering and pain are integral to life's experience but they need not humiliate, defeat, and destroy us! A *Detroit News* article some years ago carried the story of Kirk Gibson during his glory days with the Tigers. Few really knew the price of pain and agony paid by Gibson for that glory.

According to the article, Kirk Gibson is a baseball player who knows how to live with pain. In 1980, he tore the cartilage in his wrist. Two years later, he had a sore left knee, a strained left calf muscle, and a severe left wrist sprain. In 1983, he was out for knee surgery, and in 1985 he required 17 stitches after getting hit in the mouth with a wild pitch. In addition, he bruised a hamstring muscle, injured his right heel, and suffered a sore left ankle. His worst injury involved severe ligament damage to his ankle in 1986, a year predicted to be his best. When asked about pain, Gibson was quoted as saying, "There are pluses and minuses in everything we do in life. But the pluses for my career, myself, and my family make it worth it. It's the path I chose."

The fact that there is no gain without pain is evidence in other walks of life as well. But never is the potential payoff greater than when a person chooses to suffer with Christ in order to help others and to honor God.

With the coming of Jesus, the experience of human suffering was transformed into a glorious event! Suffering and pain need not be our taskmasters, driving us into sniveling silence and painful submission. Jesus claimed all power over it and we too possess the spiritual wherewithal to rise above it. Adversity is often our strongest ally in being tried by the fires of human suffering. As a person in my congregation who died with AIDS, who is spotlighted in my book *Street Corner Theology* remarked, "The closer we move to God, the more we master our pain."

Some time ago a fascinating article appeared in *Reader's Digest*, telling about a most unusual tree called the "Bristlecone Pine." Growing in the western mountain regions, sometimes as high as two or more miles above sea level, these evergreens may live for thousands of years. The older specimens often have only one thin layer of bark on their trunks. Considering the habitat of these trees, such as rocky areas where the soil is poor and precipitation is slight, it seems almost incredible that they should live so long or even survive at all. The environmental "adversities," however, actually contribute to their longevity. Cells that are produced as a result of these perverse conditions are densely arranged, and many resin canals are formed within the plant. Wood that is so structured continues to live for an extremely long period of time. The author Darwin Lambert says in his article, "Bristlecone Pines in richer conditions grow faster, but die earlier and soon decay." The harshness of their surroundings, then, is a vital factor in making them strong and sturdy. How similar this is to the experience of the Christian who graciously accepts the hardships God allows to come into his life. In Hebrews 12:11 we read that such chastening produces "the peaceable fruit of righteousness." (KJV)

For those not rooted in Christ, suffering can be decimating. As Christians we claim glory out of suffering.

Second, **we claim victory out of defeat. Before claiming victory we must surrender to Christ**. How strange! How paradoxical! In the battles of life, surrender precedes defeat. In the Christian life, surrender to Christ precedes victory and victory issues out of defeat! Pure, complete, unconditional surrender is the first step to Christian victory!

The crucifixion of Christ was one magnificent defeat — so thought the persons responsible for executing him! Christ died a horrifying death on a cross of shame. But with a further cross examination we discover that he turned that cross into a crown, that defeat into a victory, because he had surrendered his life to God. After the crucifixion comes the resurrection.

When asked how she got over, sister Sadie Jones said that she claimed her power through the blood of the lamb: a blood that redeems, a blood that cleanses; a blood that renews, a blood that empowers; a blood that gives you a new joy, a new power, a new purpose. Victory through defeat is the watchword of faithful Christians. The paradox is that spilled blood means death; but His spilled blood means life. The paradox is that blood spilled is the source of new life.

Claiming victory through defeat only means that you have overcome the tyrannizing, terrorizing forces of life itself; that you have cast out all fear; that not even the jaws of defeat and death can steal your crown of victory or take your song of joy.

When asked why she lived so victoriously, a saint of the church said, "Because the scriptures say, 'And it came to pass,' which means that it didn't come to stay. That's why the prayer says, 'Yea though I walk through the valley,' because *I'm coming through, I'm claiming my victory right now in the name of Jesus!*"

Many people in Seattle, Washington, are amazed at the faith and victory of little Brianne Kliner. She was one of the children poisoned by E. coli bacteria after eating a hamburger from a Jack in the Box restaurant. As she lay dying in the hospital room, many said that her mother should choose to have the doctors pull the plug, that all hope was lost since the other children poisoned had died. But that mother held on to her faith and said, "I am claiming victory right now in the name of Jesus," and now that child is out of the coma.

Claiming the victory is holding on to hope, love, and faith of Christ through personal suffering and crisis, knowing God will see you through somehow! It is living as conquerors, not as the conquered. It is trusting in God and holding on to God's unchanging hand at all times, good and bad. He who loses shall find. He who finds shall lose.

How is it that many people have lost the battle before it's begun, unfurled the flag of defeat and despair on the battleground of life's experiences before the bugles blast?

I recall reading in Civil War history the account of the Battle of Chickamauga, where soldiers marched a long way to battle. Sometimes the march is longer than the fight. If we can keep up the march and claim the victory we shall have passed through!

> *It matters not how deep entrenched the wrong*
> *How hard the battle goes, the day, how long,*
> *Faint not, fight on! Tomorrow comes the song!*

Claiming victory through defeat is like the eagle who turns the storm cloud into a chariot: An eagle sits on a crag and watches the sky as it is filling with blackness, and the forked lightnings are raging up and down. He is sitting perfectly still ... until he begins to feel the burst of the breeze and knows the hurricane has struck him. Then he swings his breast to the storm and uses the storm to go to the sky. Away he goes, borne upward by it. That is what God wants of his children: to turn storm clouds into chariots; to become victors amid adversity; to spread the wings of spirituality and trust amid the cosmic gales of life's terrifying forces.

That's how Charles Albert Tindley when he wrote "Stand By Me" could hear the storms raging in his own life and turned them into beautiful music. "When the storms of life are raging, stand by me, when the wind is tossing me like a ship upon the sea, thou who rulest wind and water, stand by me." His granddaughter, Mrs. Anderson, attests to the struggle that inspired his beautiful music.

Victory out of defeat is the hallmark of the Christian, and much of this can be fostered in the preparation of the right attitude and by cultivating a strong spiritual life. He who loses shall find. He who finds shall lose.

What allows the ship to survive the storms of the high seas? Some say the captain! Some say the crew! Some say the ocean! Some say the make of the timber which comprises the boat! The preparation that has gone into growing the timber which makes up the wood of the bow and stern. The way the sun shines on the tree. The way the soil nurtures the tree. The way the rain falls upon the tree. The way the ax is laid to the tree. The way that tree is carried out of the wilderness. The way the craftsmen care for its grain and prepare it to be shaped into the ship which allows it to survive the brutal batterings of high wind assaults on the turbulent, tumultuous seas!

What about you this morning: From what tree are you cut; what is the grain of your wood; what kind of timber are you? Can you survive the storms? Are you a tree or a post? A tree gives life and grows. A post withers and dies!

Are you getting the sunlight of prayer? Are you planted in the soil of hope and showered by the cool waters and rains of love and spirituality? Have the axes of doubt been laid to your trunk? Have no fear, for the master carpenter is here. He'll take your stump and make it into a house. He'll take your trunk and make it into a sight worth beholding.

Victory out of seeming defeat is one paradox of Christian spirituality people have difficulty comprehending.

But God with Christ instituted a new plan with a new man. Where the blind would see, the deaf would hear, the dumb would speak, the cast down would be lifted up, the lame would walk, and the demon possessed would be freed from their imprisonments. Where victory would be claimed over the forces of evil, destruction, and death! He who loses shall find. He who finds shall lose.

If you've gone through divorce, claim the victory. If you've experienced hardship from co-workers on your job, claim the victory! If you've been cast down, disappointed, disjointed, call in the anointed of God and claim the victory right now in the name of Jesus! Whatever your condition or predicament, you have the power to claim the victory by not allowing the cries of cynicism and despair to cloud your mental skies.

God's children never go down in defeat because they have an advocate, a savior, a counselor, a liberator! Victory through defeat is the watchword of faithful Christians. Just when the world is counting you out, Jesus is counting you in. Just when others say that you are finished, that's when Jesus says, "We're just getting started." Just when you thought there was no way out, you discover a way in, a way into his blessings, a way into his mercy, a way into his joy, a way into his promises, a way into God's son. We turn our defeats into victories and count it all joy.

Finally, the third paradox is **gain through loss. He who loses shall find. He who finds shall lose.** Most people count loss as loss, not as gain, but the beloved of God know that every good-bye ain't gone, every closed eye ain't sleep, and every melody ain't a song.

Gain through loss! Many people spend their lives counting their losses. The investor counts his losses in the stock market. The army general counts his losses in battle. Statisticians, morticians, and politicians count their losses in the polling places and funeral parlors of the nation.

But Christians turn losses into gains. It's not what I've lost, but what I've gained. Not what's been taken, but what's been given. Not how much I don't have, but how much I do have for the remainder of the journey.

Judith Viorst's classic work *Necessary Losses* reveals how life is a series of experiences wherein we are losing and gaining. Intrinsic to life are processes by which we detach, separate, and lose things. This process is central to our growth as it is to life itself. But some losses are harder to deal with, like the loss of a child, or someone dear before they've had a chance to enjoy life to the fullest. All life is a process of adjustments to unions and separations, losses and gains.

Loss too often becomes a definition of our capacity and character as the people of God. Loss is not a definition of our persona but a description of our condition.

But even here the experience of Jesus is significant. For he has taken the cross and turned it into a crown, taken our defeats and despair and turned them into victory and joy. Our Lord specializes in turning our pain into purpose, our doubt into decisions, and our losses into dividends.

I don't know about you today, but I know a man who always pays good faith dividends; a man whose markets are bull instead of bear, who has more gold, more CD's — Christian determination

109

— more power and joy than all the Federal Reserves put together. I know a man who turns everything he touches to gold; a junk man who doesn't sell junk bonds, but will take the junk of your life, the old discarded, unwanted, dilapidated, misused and abused parts of your soul and turn them into blue chip, hallelujah, better than Wall Street, Dow Jones, Nikkei averages; a man who is chairman of my board; a man who will turn the least that you have into the best and greatest for God. His name is Jesus!

For the old is made new, the lost is found, the weak are made strong, the hurt are made healthy, the lonely are comforted, the blind are given sight, the lame walk, the hopeless are given hope, the loveless find love, and the powerless are given new power! He'll turn your windfall misfortunes into inflation-free spirituality. He'll underwrite your franchise and give you hallelujah joy. He'll take whatever you give and give whatever you take. He's got more gold than Fort Knox. More oil than the Rockefellers. More power than the Trilateral Commission. His name is Jesus! He'll turn your losses into gains and make you a new person. Just trust him. Just invest in him and your returns will be marvelous! Because of our faith and the power imparted by Jesus, we are able to take situations that would ordinarily devastate and decimate and turn them into victorious possibilities. This has much to do with attitude, prayer, and a deepening and abiding spirituality whose practice both strengthens and guides us through the maze and craze of human life.

Small wonder why people are amazed at the staying power of Christians, the praying power of Christians, for they are able to take the paradoxes of life and change them into victories for Christ!

For we take glory out of suffering, victory out of defeat, and gain out of loss!

> His name is Jesus ...
> For he's my
> Alpha and Omega
> Holy lamb of God
> Horn of Salvation
> Desire of all Nations

Rock in a Weary Land
Bright and Morning Star
Good Shepherd
Amazing Grace
Sure Foundation
King of Kings
Perfect Purifier
Mighty Fortress
Dayspring from on High
Comforter, Counselor, Creator and Liberator
My heart regulator
My mind intimator
My joy, my hope, my love, my all in all.

For he'll make
The stingy give up
The dirty wash up
The guilty fess up
The lame stand up
The childish grow up
The foolish wise up
The dead raise up
The lost show up
The mute speak up
The halt step up
The convicted shut up
The sleeping wake up
The wounded bind up
The slow speed up and the swift slow up
The saved fill up, give up, and go on up for His glory.
What a paradox!

"He who finds his life shall lose it. He who loses his life shall find it!"

Take Off The Grave Clothes!

John 11:38-44

Today our lesson paints a poignant picture of one of the most famous of Jesus' acts: raising Lazarus from the dead. Lazarus had been a dear friend of Jesus and the scriptures say Jesus loved him and his entire family. When news reached Jesus of Lazarus' death, his heart was sorrowful. He wept inwardly and outwardly. Despite the bad news, he kept confidence that Lazarus would be raised. Despite the woeful lament the news caused for those who loved and knew Lazarus, Jesus quietly assured his disciples and Lazarus' family that a great thing would soon happen. Jesus knew that he would raise Lazarus because he loved him so and understood that his mission of convincing others of his power would be partially fulfilled by this act.

There were fellow Jews who needed to be assured of the truth and power of miracles. There were those disciples who lived with him, ate with him, walked and talked with him, and cried with him who still weren't convinced but needed to be told of the power and promise of his purpose. There were those bystanders, naysayers, and dream slayers. Those prophets of doom and gloom who had written him off as some quack with queer quirks who dispensed medicinal cures to the blind and lame through some superficial sorcery smacking of the demonic. There were princes and prelates who doubted his claims to authority. Scribes, Pharisees, and Sadducees who had written him off as a poor, homeless preacher who didn't have a pot and a window to throw it out of.

Jesus' raising of Lazarus would send them all scurrying for cover. They would see and hear and finally be convinced that he was Lord and liberator of the people of God: the despised, the rejected, the hemmed in, and the hung up. The homeless, the hapless, the hopeless, and the heartless would all be convinced that his power was one which came from on high, which could not be vanquished or diminished by the political and religious powers of his time, could not be snuffed out by the sinister cynicism of spiritual wannabes and social gonna-bes. Jesus is Lord and his raising of Lazarus drove home the fact to those in power so that they plotted all the more to crucify him.

Yes, Jesus raised Lazarus. Just as he raised the dead yesterday he can raise the dead today. For there are those living today who are like the living dead. They have lost a zeal and zest for living and life. Their souls are no longer revived by the fresh springs of living waters. They have immersed themselves in the still, stinking, stagnant stench of despair and disillusionment and no longer live life with hope, joy, and the resurrection spirit. They are the spiritually dead. The emotionally dead. The relationally dead. The vocationally dead. The psychologically dead. Those who have died to the possibilities of life.

The great Albert Schweitzer said, "It is not so much that a man dies while he lives but what dies in him as he lives."

These living dead have lost the vitality of life and describe life as the following: A joke which isn't funny. A jail sentence which we get from the crime of being born, or a disease for which the only cure is death. A tale told by an idiot, full of sound and fury, signifying nothing. Or perhaps they echo the words of multimillionaire Ted Turner on Larry King's television talk show who said, "Life is a B grade movie. You don't want to leave in the middle of it, but you don't want to see it again."

The point is many people have lost hope and have developed a pessimism and hopelessness which places them among the living dead. All this week Ed Love of WDET celebrated the life of the late, great Dizzy Gillespie who died on January 6. One thing about Diz, besides being a great musician, was his zing for life. He imparted joy through his personality and music. He had zest for life, rivaled by none.

Contrast, if you will, the vim and vigor of a Dizzy Gillespie and the morose, maudlin melancholy of Miles Davis. Both were great musicians and geniuses. But Diz had that particular flare for life which resonated a peculiar spark that put a twinkle in your eye and endeared him to millions of fans over the world.

Jesus raised Lazarus and Jesus can raise us so that we might reclaim the experience of being alive, so that we may be filled with a joy and enthusiasm for living unsurpassed.

Joan Benny, the daughter of Jack Benny, said her father had a love of life which was infectious to those around him. He loved life and lived it to the hilt.

The prophet Ezekiel when confronted with the dry, lifeless bones in the valley was called upon to revive the dead bones. Yes, these bones can live!

It is important to remember that Jesus raised Lazarus, and Jesus can raise us. But equally significant is what Jesus said to the people who observed the raising of Lazarus, something as important as the resurrection itself. After raising Lazarus up and giving him new life, he commanded the people around him to "take off the grave clothes and let him go."

You see, it is not enough to be raised and given a new lease on life. It is not enough to be transformed and transfigured from the living dead to the living. It is not enough to relinquish one condition for another: death for life, or hopelessness for hopefulness. It is not enough for God to liberate us from one particular set of habits, to be freed from sin and guilt and despair; we must take off the grave clothes and be let go, loosed, forever freed from the burdens which bind and obliterate the last vestiges of light and life in us!

Taking off the grave clothes was just as important in Lazarus' new life of freedom as the act of being raised itself.

You see many people are freed, liberated, saved, unbound, resurrected, emancipated from being spiritually dead to being fully alive, but they still have on their grave clothes. So long as they have them on they can never be truly set free.

Our resurrection must be succeeded by a final unraveling of those garments of restraint and constraint which still bind us and keep us prisoner.

I have observed many people temporarily freed from a particular set of destructive habits, such as alcoholism, drug addiction, spousal abuse, marital infidelity, thievery, dishonesty, chronically low self-esteem and self-doubt, only to return to the same practices because they and those around them have not taken off the grave clothes of defeat, despair, disillusionment, and disbelief.

Edwin Friedman in his work, *Generation to Generation*, tells how in many instances a particular family member is freed from some debilitating habit or way of living, only to return to the family to take the problems right back up. They have experienced a resurrection, but their grave clothes have not been removed. Part of the problem, says Friedman, is that those individuals return to a family environment which unwittingly enables or facilitates the problem.

He says rather than remove the individual and give him or her therapy, the entire family should go into counseling and therapy to explore ways in which they are helping to create the problem. It is not enough to be resurrected; the further step of removing the grave clothes is needed for the restoration of health and human wholeness and recovering the experience of being fully alive and vital.

Removing the grave clothes simply means taking away those things, those elements, those obstacles and impediments which enable continually destructive behavior. It is the failure to remove those incentives, those garments, which cause us to return to a life of the living dead. If an alcoholic is returned to a family setting, it would do the family well to remove all alcohol from the home. The entire family must engage in behavior that will allow the individual to sustain over the long haul a wholesome and healthy life. Everyone in this case must remove the grave clothes, those reminders and catalysts which compel people into self-destructive behavior.

It was not enough for Jesus to raise Lazarus. His grave clothes had to be taken off. It is not enough for us to be raised. We must remove the grave clothes which bind us to life among the spiritually dead.

We must therefore first remove the grave clothes of disbelief. Now many people have experienced the resurrecting, liberating, saving power of God, but still have on the grave clothes of disbelief. They have seen what God has done in their lives. They are living witnesses, but doubt whether God is real and truly has the power to transform and uplift lives. Despite what God has done to change their lives and those around them, they still doubt whether God has the power to redeem through God's sanctifying grace. They still ponder the power and possibilities of God after being resurrected or saved or snatched from the jaws of death. They still allow the hounds of disbelief to stalk and rout them into never-ending cynicism, pessimism, and despair.

The grave clothes of disbelief must be removed, not by him who is resurrected, but by those who have seen and heard it.

One former inmate related his struggle to break free from the bonds of crime. Fifteen years of his life were spent in prison. It suddenly dawned upon him that if he was going to change his life he had better not go back to the community in which he always got into trouble. He decided to accept Christ and be saved, resurrected from the dead, but more importantly, he decided to take off his grave clothes by not returning to the place of his discontent. He turned disbelief into belief and transformed not only his situation but his life condition into something positive.

Once you've experienced resurrection, you must do all you can to sustain the experience of being alive in Christ, and this means removing the grave clothes.

The grave clothes of despair and defeat must also be removed. There are countless people whose entire lives are defined, shaped, by one traumatic experience.

The successes and failures of their entire lives revolve around this one incident or series of instances. The result is they have stopped living. They live their lives not as victors but as despairing defeatists. They have put on the garments of despair and defeat. They continue to don the grave clothes of hopelessness. Their entire lives are spent living among the tombs.

Despair and defeat are the twin engines of our spiritual power failures. Jesus resurrects the dead so that hope may reign, that love may enthrone, and that victory may be shared among the people of God.

Many people are still enshrouded with defeatist attitudes. God has worked miracles in their lives and has granted them their hearts' desire. God has loved them, honored them, adored them, and held back his merciful wrath in times when punishment and banishment from the family of God were warranted. God's love has lifted them. God's grace has enabled them. God's justice has liberated them. God's peace has calmed them. God's mercy has quickened them. God's joy has prompted them. God's salvation has made them new creatures in life, and they still manage through it all to have an attitude of defeat and despair. You know these persons. They have everything. More than enough twelve times over, and they are still living in the grave clothes of defeat. They have everything and nothing at the same time. God has given them everything and they still can't claim the victory because they are stuck in quagmires, the quicksands, of despair and defeat.

Take off the grave clothes of despair and defeat. Your God is a God of life, a God of power, a God of love, a God of redemption, a God of grace, a God of the resurrection where joy, wholeness, life, and vitality are restored so that life in all of its aliveness can be experienced and lived. Those who follow Christ have already claimed the victory in following him!

I know a woman named Mary Casselberry who has breast cancer. Not a word of lament, not a word of regret, not a word of despair, not a word of defeat, and not a word of hopelessness has ever issued from her lips. She is living victoriously, triumphantly, in the midst of what could be a despairing situation. When asked, "How are you doing?" she says, "I'm blessed." When asked, "How long?" she says, "Not long." When asked, "How far?" she says, "God has brought me a mighty long way." She has not only experienced the resurrecting love of Christ, but has gone further by discarding the grave clothes of despair and doubt. Despite a life-threatening disease, she has found the strength to stand up and shed the grave clothes of defeat and despair which could result from breast cancer!

Finally, those of us who would experience this new life, this new vitality, this new resurrecting power must shed the grave clothes of disillusionment. God did not bring you this far to leave you. God is not a here-today-and-gone-today God. God did not call you to be God's very own in order to disown that which is

God's. "Disillusionment" broken down means: dis, ill, us, ion, ment. That is, you believe that whatever goes wrong is intended, designed, especially for you, to bring you illness, disenchantment, and disillusionment, which lead to disengagement from the will and work of God.

But God is not the co-signer of calamity and confusion. God does not disillusion us so that we might live our lives on the jagged edge of despair. God is a resurrecting God, a liberating God, a God of grace and glory.

Take off your grave clothes, Lazarus! Take off your grave clothes, sinner! Take off your grave clothes, defeatist! Take off your grave clothes, disillusionist! Take off your grave clothes, despairer! Take off your grave clothes, disbeliever! God has a new life for you. God wants you to live your life in the fullness of God's goodness and glory. God wants the best for you. Take those grave clothes off. Stop looking at the downside and get with the upside. Stop looking at the minus column and get your life into the credit column. Stop looking at the glass half empty. Start tasting from a cup that runneth over.

For I have never seen the righteous forsaken or a seed begging bread. Live your life and live it with all the zest, zeal, zing, and zip that you can muster. Come out of your grave clothes! Take the next step to resurrection, rebirth, and renewal to seal your life in the power and glow of his liberating and saving grace.

Shed therefore the garments of hopelessness, powerlessness, lovelessness, friendlessness, and godlessness, and put on the crown of joy and salvation!

Come out of those grave clothes, for you are a child of the king. You are spiritual royalty. All power is held in the hands of him who sent his son for you. Come out of the grave clothes of "I can't do it," for in Christ all things are possible. Stop looking for reasons to die, and find reasons to live. Trade in that cross for a crown and live life in all of its fullness, wholeness, and vitality. You are a child of the king. Take off the grave clothes and go free!

The African Foundations Of Christianity

Exodus 4:1-7

In surveying the vast and rich history of African-American people, we must go beyond the shores of America to the continent of "Alkebulan" or Africa. We are indebted to the late Dr. Carter G. Woodson and members for the study of Negro Life and History for designating February as a time for observing the outstanding contributions of black people, not only to American but also to world history.

A great tragedy of our times is that many people, both black and white, think that Black History began four hundred years ago in what Kenneth Stampp called "The Peculiar Institution" of slavery. Yet, when we diligently and painstakingly research our history, we see that it began before Europe was Europe, and before Western civilization had reached its present oasis.

In fact, when we rightfully and truthfully survey history, we see that African peoples in the Nile Valley civilization of Egypt were responsible for developing complex cosmological and theological systems; were instrumental in creating mathematics, mortuary science, aeronautical engineering, architectural science (of which the pyramids remain magnificent testaments), methods of birth control, the sciences of mechanical and agricultural engineering, botany, chemistry, philosophy, music, drama, metallurgy, and even religion. These and other disciplines were first articulated and cultivated by Nile Valley Africans. In his celebrated work *Ruins of Empires*, Count C.F. Volney made the following observation in 1789:

> *To think that a race of Black men and women who are*
> *today our slaves and the object of our contempt are the*

121

*same ones to whom we owe our arts, sciences and the
very use of speech.*[1]

Volney, as other white explorers of previous German, French,
and English expeditions, had discovered the truth about Africa and
Egypt's role and influence on the development of Western civilization. Many of the white explorers found the idea of Egypt, then
considered the cradle of civilization, being ruled by black Africans as disturbing and repulsive. Napoleon Bonaparte, upon ar-
riving in Egypt with garrisons of conquering soldiers, ordered his
cannon battalion to blow off the nose of the Sphinx because of its
African features.

In further corroborating the role of black Africans in giving
the world its first systems of thought, Count C.F. Volney tells us:

> *These are a people now forgotten discovered while oth-
> ers were yet barbarians, the elements of the arts and sci-
> ences. A race of men now rejected from society for their
> sable skin and woolly hair, founded on the study of the
> laws of nature those civil and religious systems which
> still govern the universe.*[2]

During the nineteenth century, when British imperialism and
white racism reached their greatest heights, many European nations under the aegis of the ruling classes sponsored excavations
of Africa. Egyptologists, archaeologists, geologists, and anthropologists all converged on major projects in Egypt and parts of
North and Central Africa to discover the truth about the beginnings of civilization.

At this time many schools for research of ancient history and
culture were formally organized. James Henry Breasted founded
the Oriental Institute at the University of Chicago. British and
French schools and museums were also founded. Schools were
also organized at Harvard and Princeton, which sponsored archaeo-
logical expeditions.

The problem with many of the excavations and the subsequent
histories written on the projects and their findings was that many

of the artifacts and relics discovered at these sites in Egypt contained the busts and heads of people with distinctively African or Negroid features. This posed a problem for many of the white racists who had been taught from day one that white people had created what is known today as Western culture and civilization. As a result, many of the artifacts which were unearthed were deliberately and maliciously defaced and even destroyed because of their typical African characteristics of broad noses and thick lips.

Thus a great conspiracy began on the banks of the Nile and continues to this very day — a conspiracy to erase and eradicate the truth about black people's contribution to the development of the Nile Valley culture, civilization, and subsequent world history.

As Martin Bernal tells us in his great work *Black Athena*, many excavations were sponsored by people and governments bent on preserving the myth of white superiority and the Aryan creation of civilization.[3] The discovery of artifacts with distinctively African characteristics flew in the face of everything these white scholars had been taught about their history and culture. The great African scholar Cheikh Anta Diop reminds us that, "It is necessary to reconcile African Civilization with the history which Europe distorted in order to deny both the accomplishment of African History and the reality of our humanity."[4]

Throughout America and Europe, myths have been propagated that African peoples made no contribution to world history. A leading white historian, Arnold Toynbee, incredibly and myopically observed that the only people who had contributed anything of value to the world were white and yellow peoples. Toynbee goes as far as developing a hierarchy of peoples whose contributions were of greatest value, thus placing whites at the top.

Regrettably, such lies and myths have been touted as truth, and nowhere are they more manifest than in the field of religion, particularly in the founding and development of Christianity and the Judaeo-Christian heritage. Small wonder that there remains such a great conspiracy to divest Egypt of all black African influence since this is the birthplace of the Jewish and Christian faiths. Herodotus, the so-called Greek "father of history," describes the Egyptians as: "The Colchians, Egyptians and Ethiopians have thick lips, broad noses, woolly hair and they are burnt of skin."[5] Herodotus made this statement over 2,500 years ago and there is no reason to believe it to be false. He was writing as an eyewitness, and because of Egypt's outstanding contributions to world culture as a black nation, a great effort has been afoot to remove any semblance of a black presence from it. This is especially true when considering that Egypt is the foundation of the Jewish and Christian religions.

James Henry Breasted, whom we mentioned earlier as the founder of the Oriental Institute, and who was no staunch supporter of the idea of a black Egypt, made the following statement:

> *The ripe social and moral development of mankind in the Nile Valley which is three thousand years older than that of the Hebrews contributed essentially to the formation of Hebrew Literature which we call the Old Testament.*[6]

If we are to discover the African basis of Christianity, we must go to the Old Testament and the life and culture of the Hebrew people who are the spiritual ancestors of Christians. The Hebrew people lived hundreds of years (possibly more) in black Egypt and borrowed many of their moral, spiritual, and religious precepts and concepts from Nile Valley Africans. Although Egypt is much maligned in Hebraic literature as an oppressive nation, its influence on the formation of Hebrew literature and culture is unmistakable. This may explain why there is such a concerted effort to remove, ignore, and negate the role of Egypt in the formation of Judaism and Christianity. To acknowledge indebtedness to Egypt as a positive influence in the formation of Hebraic and later Israelite culture would be to affirm the positive influence of black people in the development of these world religions. This explains why scholars and historians still ridiculously attempt to speak of Egypt as a Middle Eastern rather than an African nation — to divorce any notion of the nation being authentically black — African.

Even in the creation story of the Hebrews in the book of Genesis, particularly 2:10-14, the Garden of Eden is mentioned as being near a river that runs through or near the area of Cush, which is another name for Ethiopia.

As S.B. and Louis Leakey and other anthropologists have discovered, all evidence points to Africa as the birthplace of humankind. A description of the Egyptian god Amen even mirrors characteristics of the Hebrew and Christian God:

> *... The priests of Amen were never tired of proclaiming the greatness and majesty of Amen ... they appealed to Him, as to a loving father, in their troubles and sickness, being persuaded that the human side of him could feel, sympathize, understand their difficulties. To these he was merciful, kind, gracious and forgiving. He protected the weak against the strong, and the oppressed against the oppressor. He honored the humble, strengthened the weak, healed the sick, fed the poor and needy, protected the orphan, relieved the widow and assisted every one who called on his name in distress.*[7]

Then the god Amen was synthesized with Ra, which means "light," and thus the word, "Amen-Ra." The two principal features of Egyptian spirituality and religion which are important for us to remember today are that Spirit is breath — Kha Ba — and that Spirit is light.

In understanding the Holy Spirit today we must therefore go back to its African foundations. Although current Christian ideas of the Holy Spirit bear marked differences from their Egyptian predecessors, the similarities remain obvious.

For the Egyptians, the creative, sustaining spirit of life as congenitally embodied in the creator God's construction of the universe is manifest through the power and workings of nature. An Egyptian synonym for God was "netchter," whose English equivalent is the word "nature." Thus similarities exist between man and his spirit nature; his creative, procreative capacities in nature; and the divine breath which infuses all of life with existence in nature. Finally, Budge tells us:

> *All evidence collected by Sethe (a fellow Egyptologist)*
> *proves undoubtedly that in the later period of Egyptian*
> *History "Amen" was regarded as the "breath of life"*
> *and the spirit which permeated and vivified everything.*
> *He was, "Suh en ankh, der hauch des lebens" and*
> *pneuma of the Greeks. Sethe thinks that the creating wind*
> *which was over the waters of Nunu and the Spirit of God*
> *which moved on the face of the waters have so much in*
> *common that Yahweh (God of Hebrews) and Amen (God*
> *of Egyptians) is identical with Amen. He points out that,*
> *at a later period, the Spirit of God of the book of Genesis*
> *became an independent being under the form of the Holy*
> *Ghost of Christianity.*[8]

Other Hebrew borrowings from black Africa are temple worship, the Ark of the Covenant, praise music in worship, readings from sacred texts, and other religious rituals too numerous to name here. James Bonwick offers a description of a typical Egyptian worship service hundreds, perhaps thousands, of years before the Christian Church was formally established:

> *Processions were a leading feature of Egyptian church*
> *service, the cross bearer led the way, followed by the*
> *shrine bearers, priests, singers and musicians. The Holy*
> *Box or Ark was the prominent object.*[9]

Note that the cross was used as a symbol of worship long before Christianity was formally organized, which is further corroboration of an African influence on the Christian faith by way of symbols.

Furthermore, in considering the significant role of leadership for the Hebrews and later Israelites, we must remember Moses was Egyptian and grew up in "pharaoh's court." A possible hint of his African physiognomy is raised by the following passage of scripture. (Read Exodus 4:1-7.)

In this scripture God is trying to prove a point to Moses about God's infinite and miraculous power. God first changes a stick into a snake and then asks Moses to put his hand into his bosom.

In taking his hand out it is "white as snow." (KJV) In placing his hand back into his bosom, "It is restored as the rest of his flesh." The question is now raised, what was the rest of his flesh? If God used an extreme example by changing an inanimate object — a stick — into an animate moving snake, why would he not use the same extremes in further proving his point by changing the color of his skin to the extreme opposite of what it originally was? The conclusion is that his skin must have been black, if we utilize the same logic.

Not only does this text raise a question about Moses' appearance, but in Numbers 12:1 we find that he had made people angry by marrying a Cushite woman. We stated earlier that Cush is another name for "Ethiopia." Their anger was not kindled because she was black but because she was of another nationality — Ethiopian. Since the Ethiopians are revered as the progenitors of Egyptians, to marry an Ethiopian may have been considered betrayal, especially since the Hebrews were trying to rid themselves of everything Egyptian after the Exodus.

Some scholars, in an attempt to remove the African vestiges of these Hebraic texts, often dismiss Moses' marrying an Ethiopian woman as an anomaly or freak occurrence. Josef Ben Jochannan and others have suggested that African influences can be seen even in the Ten Commandments, which Jochannan believes were an abbreviated version of the Egyptian 147 Negative Confessions.[10]

Forty-two of the 147 Negative Confessions were derived from the Egyptian *Coffin Texts* centuries before Moses received the Ten Commandments on Mount Sinai. For example: Confessions 1 and 2 read as follows: I have not committed sin; I have not committed robbery with violence. Confessions 4 and 7 read as follows: I have not slain men and women; I have not stolen property from God.

Despite the stark similarities between the Hebrew Ten Commandments and the Egyptian Negative Confessions, the Sinai experience of Moses represented a break from the Egyptian understanding of how God revealed himself in the lives of His people. The symbol of the Golden Calf or Bull which the Hebrews worshipped at the foot of Sinai, when Moses was receiving the Commandments, was an Egyptian sacred symbol. Many other instances can be cited of Egyptian remnants in the practice of Old Testament faith.

Even in the New Testament we have African influences in the formation of Hellenistic or Greco-Roman culture. C.L.R. James' *Stolen Legacy* clearly outlines the African influences on Greek philosophy. Aristotle, Plato, and other Greek philosophers took much of their learning from the North Africans. It is believed that Plato modeled his famous "Academy" on the schools of Egypt and Luxor.

In modern times Albert Schweitzer developed the "Quest of The Historical Jesus." This was an attempt by numerous scholars to discover the historical Jesus. Who was he? What did he look like? We know much about the Christ of faith, but who was this man Jesus? Can we know anything about him?

Much to both the liking and dismay of many of his colleagues, Schweitzer called off this quest, warning that the Jesus we discover may not be the one we are looking for.

A German scholar, Robert Eisler, in his work *The Messiah Jesus and John The Baptist*, gives a startling description of the historical Jesus based upon the historian Josephus' account and the trial records of Pontius Pilate.[11]

Jesus is described as "melagchrous," which is a derivative of the Greek word "Black." Melagchrous means "Black or dark skinned." Here is further evidence of the conspiracy to remove any hint of an African presence. This may be a clue to why Schweitzer called off his quest and then left Europe to set up a mission hospital in French Equatorial Africa. Schweitzer understood that such information could potentially destroy the foundation of Western society which was principally laid on the religion of Christianity. How could white people justify the myth of white superiority and continue to colonize and enslave African people on the premise of inherent inferiority when their very Jesus himself may have been a black man?

We cannot possibly exhaust all evidence of the African foundation of Christianity, but this provides an intriguing start to an ongoing debate about black people's influence in the formation of Christianity.

1. Count C.F. Volney, *Ruins of Empires* (Paris, 1789), pp. 16-17.

2. *Ibid.,* pp. 16-17.

3. Martin Bernal, *Black Athena, Volume I, The Fabrication of Ancient Greece* (New Brunswick, New Jersey: Rutgers University Press, 1987).

4. See Cheikah Anta Diop's *The African Origin of Civilization* (Westport, Conn.: Lawrence Hill, 1974); *Precolonial Black Africa* (Westport, Conn.: Lawrence Hill, 1987); *The Cultural Unity of Black Africa* (Chicago: Third World Press, 1978).

5. Herodotus, *Histories* (London: 1848), p. 122.

6. James Henry Breasted, *The Dawn of Conscience* (New York: Charles Scribner's Sons, 1934), p. xv.

7. E.A. Wallis Budge, *From Fetishism To God in Ancient Egypt* (New York: Dover Publications, 1988), pp. 168-169.

8. *Ibid.,* p. 170.

9. James Bonwick, *Egyptian Belief and Modern Thought* (London: African Publication Society, 1983), p. 368.

10. Josef Ben Jochannan, *Africa: Mother of Western Civilization* (New York: Alkebulan Books, 1966).

11. Robert Eisler, *The Messiah Jesus and John The Baptist* (London: Methuen and Company, 1931).

African-American Spirituality: The African's Gift To America

Exodus 3:1-10

As we commence celebrations of Black History this month, I want to say what a wonderful thing that we have time for formal observances of the great contributions black people have made to world civilization in general and to America in particular. We are a great people who have literally and spiritually come a long, long way. We have built the pyramids and originated the mathematical, medical, and physical sciences. We invented the first alphabet and gave to humanity its first language and systems of civil and political government. We have made our mark in literature and letters. Our writers range from Socrates and Aesop to William Shakespeare, Alexandre Dumas, and Alexander Pushkin;from Ralph Ellison to Toni Morrison; from Cheikh Anta Diop to W.E.B. DuBois and Carter G. Woodson. We are a people of music, culture, and industry. We have among us Ludwig van Beethoven and Franz Joseph Haydn as well as Harry Burleigh, John Coltrane, Wynton Marsalis, Marian Anderson, Kathleen Battle, and Paul Robeson.

We have built some of the greatest monuments in the world and have made some of the greatest discoveries and inventions in the world, ranging from the fountain pen to the ironing board, from the electric lamp to lubricators for steam engines and intricate systems of refrigeration. We have built highways, byways, and bridges on American soil. We have fought America's wars and won her medals. Our sweat, blood, and brawn laid the economic foundation of America's capitalist system, and our mothers and grandmothers nursed white babies while our men bore the brunt of the overseer's lash while working from "can't see to can't see." While our gifts to America are vast and varied, one of our greatest gifts is our spirituality, for it is the raw material, the vital impetus, the true substance, which has fueled our souls and lives and has sustained us through the trials and troubles of the American experience.

As an African-American, who unapologetically and unashamedly celebrates the life, history, and culture of his people, I want to say that I love my country. I love America. Robert Hutchins, former president of the University of Chicago, once observed that the university is not a very good place, but it is the best there is. Some might say that of America. For some, America may not be a very good place. But it's the very best place on earth. America is not a perfect place, but there is no better place. There are some things I do not like about my country: its racism, its hatred, and its injustice; the way it throws away its old people and idolizes youth. I disdain the polarization of human groups around issues which ultimately have no value, because we have more in common than indifference. I don't like those things which separate and alienate people and bring out the worst in them, but I still love my country and am not ashamed to say that. This does not mean that in our love we ignore the things which hound, plague, and discomfit us. It only means that we must all work harder to help our nation realize its true potential. It means focusing on the positive, the strengths, and using them as points of bringing all of us together rather than means of alienating us further.

What nation is as diverse as America? What other country on earth can boast of giving experiences to so many people of so many different lineages and racial and ethnic backgrounds? You can't go to any other country on earth, be it Japan or Germany or even our northern neighbor Canada, and see the diversity of people in government, in business, and in other aspects of the nation's life. The great Howard Thurman said that the American experiment was the very mind of God doing a new thing in human history. I love America. Because I have traveled in other parts of the world, I have seen the poverty. I have seen the decadence. I have seen the repression. America is not a perfect place; it's just the best place there is, and as an African-American I am not ashamed to say that I love my country. What makes America great is that various people can contribute the best they have to make the whole better. The great challenge of America in the future is to allow each group of people to do what it does best and make its contribution for the betterment of the whole.

Although Africans came to America under debilitating and excruciating circumstances, and endured the horrors and terrors of slavery and later Jim Crow, we are still here, still striving with all our wits and guts to make our land a better place. We're still here, striving to be all that we can be. Striving to make ourselves and others around us better, and we are not ashamed to make positive statements of worth our people have made in making America great.

Several weeks ago, after preaching a sermon on the positive principles of Kwanzaa and about the need to build our people up and strive to set standards of excellence, I received a card from an irate listener who castigated me for preaching racism over the air. All I did was say some positive things about our people and encourage them to keep looking up and lifting each other up by practicing Kwanzaa not just in December but every day during the year. This response totally misinterpreted what I said. But it corroborated something I knew already: that however positive you are in helping your people, there are some people who will take what you say and twist it for the worst, for there is something in them that cannot grasp black people saying something good about themselves. The whole tone of the note was to place me on the defensive, to make me apologize for saying the positive things about my people, which is something I will never stop doing. Such people are so quick to cast blame. But they don't realize that this preacher is unapologetically helping his people become the best they can be. I don't need to apologize to anybody for making positive statements nor do I need to get permission from anyone to do so. Every other group can do whatever it wants to enhance and empower its community and it presents no problem, but the moment we do something positive to make our people better and not bitter, to make positive strides to help our people be the best that they can be so that America can be the best that it can be, certain people have problems. If you've got a problem, turn the channel, but don't ever expect me to stop saying the positive things to make our people better citizens and better human beings, better businessmen and better politicians, better husbands and better wives, better fathers and better mothers, better entrepreneurs and better builders for the future.

Today, I want to uplift our people again by talking about the positive aspects of African-American spirituality. I stated that African-American spirituality had been one of our greatest gifts to America. It is the one thing we possess which has allowed us to sustain ourselves through the difficult times of life in America. It has been a positive contribution, not only to us but to America as a whole. It also conferred upon us a sense of positive identity and encouraged us to be the best that we can be in all things by setting standards of excellence in an environment which potentially threatens to bring out the worst in us.

Black spirituality has been our greatest gift and we must do all we can to nurture and sustain that gift as we move into the future. African-American spirituality is not only an emblem of hope, but a guidepost for building strong and viable communities for the future. You might ask how is it so important and why is it so important.

Long ago, when our forebears came to the new land, everything was stripped from us but our spirituality. This alone sustained us through the hard times. We have always believed in God. We have always been a spiritual people who believed in a higher power and a God who controlled the universe and providence. We believed that God would bring a brighter day for our people. This belief in a higher power helped us develop a sensibility about our condition that made us hold out for a better day. We had nothing else but a firm belief that God would somehow see us through the trials and terrors of living black in America. **A hallmark of African-American spirituality is first the ability to face, adapt, and overcome the terrors of our social condition.** Our spirituality created within us a desire to go beyond the limitations placed upon us by the larger society. Our belief in God helped us to be more than just slaves. There had to be something within the belief system of the slave which allowed him to face, adapt to, and finally overcome the problems he or she faced. This has always been an important part of our spiritual belief: our ability to overcome hardship; to face trials head on and to make life better; to turn disadvantages into advantages and to claim the spiritual victory to press on towards the mark. Many scholars speak of the expressive needs of African-American spirituality, but the adaptive needs — that is the ability to face, adapt to, and overcome great odds — are an equally important element of our spiritual heritage. How could we have survived slavery and all the troubles we've faced, were it not for firm belief in a higher power? We didn't have psychologists and psychiatrists to give us therapy to cope with our condition, so there had to be something to help us through, and I say it was God, very God.

Our spirituality has equipped us with methods of problem solving and resolving which helped us get through the hard trials of life's experiences. We have always had to solve problems since our beginnings here. Many people would have us believe that we are the problem, but the truth is we have been since our beginnings here the answer to some of America's greatest problems. The creativity and genius of our spirituality have helped America get through her toughest times and we should never forget that. Our spirituality provided answers when nothing else could or would. Ever since our genesis here in America we have been used as an answer to a problem facing the nation, whether it has been working America's plantations, or working in her factories, or packing her sports arenas, or reviving failing franchises, or serving in her armed services. We have always been called upon to help solve the nation's problems and have been the answer to the problem rather than being the problem, as some would have us believe. Even Lincoln wanted to enlist black soldiers to fight the war because he knew that they would be the answer to the problem of civil strife which wrecked and wracked the nation. And whatever you say about slavery, it was instituted as an answer to a problem facing American entrepreneurs and merchants. How can we develop an economy that will make us and the nation wealthy and who can we use to do the labor to sustain that economy? Who will work our fields and build our wealth? Who will nurse our children and feed our hungry bellies? Who?

Our spirituality has taught us to overcome difficulties and has given us answers to problems facing us, because it transformed us from going-unders to over-comers, and this is the first and important fact. The first great gift of African spirituality to black people in America is the ability to face problems with great odds, to develop a spirit, a mind, and a will to overcome the barriers standing in our way. We have proven this time and time again. Who else has come from that pitiable and peculiar institution of slavery and discrimination and emerged from beneath its veil with some semblance of sanity and spirituality still intact?

A central truth about our scripture lesson in Exodus today is that Moses, in leading the Hebrews out of Africa, had to prepare them to develop a spirituality that would sustain them through the wilderness of hard times. It was a faith that allowed them to overcome the challenges of their daily encounters. And so it has been for us. Just as Moses challenged his people to redefine themselves and their potential for self-worth, our spirituality has helped us do the same.

Second, our spirituality has conferred on us a positive identity when the larger culture and society tried desperately to reduce and define us as persons of no value. A friend once told me how his daddy would always tell him that he would never be anything, that he was shiftless and worthless, but yet whenever his daddy got into a serious bind he would call on the son to help him. The son had two choices: to believe he was really shiftless and lazy based on what his daddy said, or to use his mind to analyze and draw his own conclusions about his own self-worth.

When the larger society had defined us virtually as worthless chattel, as animals, as three-fifths of a man, our spirituality defined us as children of God, as people of worth, as people possessing possibilities amid disabilities and infinite opportunities to make life better. Many of our people and those of other cultures are woefully afraid of us because the larger culture has defined us as the problem, violent, savage, and disrespectful of human life. Some of this is true, but this is not true for the great majority of us. The majority of us are law-abiding and have values which reflect the best that this nation has to offer, having been sired under conditions of constant adversity.

136

We see this problem continuing today. Many of the images of black persons in the larger media are negative. We seem virtually always to be defined as a problem rather than as a problem solver. But the negative images disseminated in the media all help to define us from a deficit perspective: as always being a people in need rather than a people of great resources. We are defined as always not quite having it together, as never fully hitting the mark, and this is because of the negative labels used to limit and define us. Once we buy into the negative mythology, we reinforce the belief with negative behavior. Our positive spirituality has always encouraged us to exceed the negative definitions, to go beyond the demeaning labels, and to develop an identity that would incite dignity, self-respect, and integrity.

African-American spirituality has developed and instilled in us a positive sense of self, and much of these values has been affirmed in the black church. This sense of self does not need to disparage or put down people of other races and cultures. It has been a positive, proactive response to the attempts by the larger culture to limit our self-worth and value. African-American spirituality does not and will not spend its energy and resources blaming or depicting other people in a negative light, but focuses on developing its own strength. When the rest of the society defined blacks as second-class citizens, the church and spirituality lifted us up as children of God, worthy of God's greatest gifts and blessings. When all others scorned us, our spirituality catapulted us beyond the crippling constraints of that rejection.

Again, the experience of Moses is pertinent here. After liberation from Egyptian bondage, the Hebrews had to fight hard not to develop a wilderness mentality, where all their strengths and gifts would be defined in terms of their limitations rather than the gifts and resources they possessed that would make them a promised land people.

Third and finally, African-American spirituality has always affirmed the expenditure of positive energy towards positive and realizable goals and aspirations. Because we have had to fight hard not to become consumed by the terrible ordeals of our experience, we have found creative ways to use our energies in a

137

positive direction. That's why worship and the creativity of black culture are so important. They allow us to take potentially negative energy and sublimate or channel it into things which will make a positive difference in our lives and those around us.

How else could we have survived our holocaust without the ability to spiritually take our energies and channel them into constructive purposes? We never could have done this without it.

The gift of African-American spirituality has been 1) our ability to face, adapt to, and overcome insurmountable odds and difficulties through unswerving faith in God; 2) the ability to retain a positive self-image in a society and culture that viewed it from a deficit perspective; and 3) the ability to take potentially negative and destructive energies and turn them into positive gains for the betterment of ourselves, our people, and the nation we live in.

Our success for the future will not only be based on how well we continue to practice that vital spirituality, but how well we instill the same values in our children and their children. As the world becomes more complex, we still need something: a faith that will sustain us through the difficult and troublesome times. We need a power to hold on to, a God to keep trust in. Our spirituality is the lifeblood of our health and vitality. We must not abandon our heritage or relinquish our faith, for if it can get us through the past, it can prepare us for the future. We must keep the faith to remain strong, get stronger, and take a rightful place as a proud and gifted people in this land.

Joy Songs, Trumpet Blasts, And Hallelujah Shouts!

Joshua 6:1-21

The Israelites have come to the end of a long, long journey. They had wandered in the wilderness for forty years and now have come to the valley of their dreams. Finally, after years of false starts, dark detours, and dashed hopes, they have come to the land which God had promised.

They could have toiled out of the wilderness in forty days, but took forty years because of discontent, disbelief, and disobedience. But now God was willing, because they were willing, to move them into a paradise oasis — a land flowing with milk and honey. There's nothing like milk and honey after years of rock salt, well water, and quail gizzard.

The people of Israel were ready to move forward because they had a new leader named Joshua. Now they were ready to be led and trusted Joshua to lead them onwards. This was a new day — a time in which God would do new things in new ways. It was a day when the old and stale, the wooden and dried-up, would give way to a new dayspring from on high. The people were ready to be led because they were tired of life in the desert. Joshua would now lead them to their appointed place in history. They would now realize all the things God had in store for them because they, learning the lessons of the past, were ready to be led. The scriptures say they had consecrated themselves before crossing the Jordan and had concentrated on the word of God as spoken to them by Joshua before setting out.

The Israelites had crossed over Jordan. They were jubilant and victorious, for a dream so long deferred had now become a reality. The scriptures say they went over on the side nearest to the city of

139

Jericho, which would be the sight of their first spiritual challenge in the promised land. You see, beloved, it is not enough to cross over. We must be ready to meet the challenges which await us once we're there. Notice I stated the sight of their first **spiritual** challenge after going into the new land. For you see, this was more than a geographical or military conquest. It was a spiritual one, for it spoke more about their relationship and trust in God than the prowess of their military might and ingenuity.

They had crossed over the River now, some two million strong. Joshua is told by God that Jericho will be delivered in the hands of his people. As Joshua nears Jericho he looks up and sees a man standing in front of him, with a drawn sword in his hand. Joshua asked him, "Are you for us or for our enemies?" "Neither, but as commander of the Lord's army I have come." Immediately Joshua fell down to his knees in reverence. The commander of the Lord's army said, "Take off your sandals; you are on holy ground." And Joshua did.

God commanded Joshua, "Command seven priests with seven trumpets of ram's horns to walk before the ark. For six days circle the city once. On the seventh day, tell the priests to march around the city seven times blowing their trumpets. When you hear them sound a long blast on the trumpets, have the people give a loud shout, then the wall of the city will collapse and every man shall go straight in."

So Joshua did as he was commanded by the Lord and called all the people together, giving them instructions on how to storm the city of Jericho.

Now Jericho, built thousands of years before Joshua was born, was one of the oldest cities in the world. Located in the wide plain of the Jordan valley about 7.5 miles northwest of the north shore of the Dead Sea and just east of the mountains of Judea, it was the epitome of Canaanite strength and invincibility. It was a mighty fortress with walls up to 25 feet high and six feet thick. Canaan's enemies were no match for it. It gave inhabitants a strong sense of security as enemies were repeatedly discomfited and stymied during times of conflict. Once behind the walls of the city, residents were safe. It was impregnable against attack and it was virtually impossible for any standing army to penetrate its formidable barriers.

Jericho was situated in fertile territory, with fresh water springs and other amenities of nature envied by many. But the Canaanites had spawned the wrath and judgment of God with their intense idol worship and evil practices. They were essentially a stronghold of rebellion against God, and the Lord promised his people that he would give them the new land. We may have all the trappings and benefits of success, but if we are not right with God, he can take it all away as he did with the Canaanites.

Joshua commanded the people as God commanded him. It was a bright, sunny day. The sky covered the fertile plains of Jordan like a blue canopy as brown, sculpted mountains of Judea peered down on the green, rolling valleys. It was a great day to claim a victory. The priests had already marched once around the city each of the six days and the people of Jericho were startled and frightened. There was excitement and commotion in the camp of the Israelites as they watched the priests lead the way from a lowly mountain's peak surrounding the valley.

The seventh day had come. The time of reckoning was here. After reaching the valley's base, the priests looked upwards to the mountain as the people began walking down into the valley towards Jericho. See them now walking briskly to take the city. They are led by Joshua, clad with a scarlet bandanna around his forehead, his hymn book in his right hand and his prayer book tucked neatly inside his shirt. Could it be the scarlet thread of Rahab the prostitute who saved the life of the Israelite spies? Joshua is the epitome of what the great Ernest Hemingway termed "grace under pressure." He is implacable and confident. He gazes the valley with an Arctic stare. While leading the people down the hill, glints of victory besparkle the eyes of those who are marching.

How strange! They march for war, but bear no arms. What nerve! They are going to battle, but have no armor! No chariots, no horses, no instruments of war! With joy songs in their hearts and trumpets resting on the shoulders of the clergy, they are walking to the tunes and shouts of a spiritual victory. "Joshua fit the battle of Jericho...." Would the same God who brought them over on dry land be the one who would give them victory as pedestrians in the valley of their enemies?

Yes, for God is doing a new thing in a new land through a new people. Each step down the mountain's slope escalates the tension of anticipation.

Meanwhile, the Canaanites are bracing themselves for the inevitable. Military garrisons have been called up on the northern, southern, and eastern flanks of the city walls. Reinforcements have been dispatched from the outposts of the northwest portion of the city, as troops march frantically to entrench themselves in their positions. Swords are brandished and sharpened. Shields and bows are passed among the troops. A large stone-throwing device is positioned on the northwest corridor of the wall as men, women, and children dash to their shelters.

Soldiers don their military garb — helmets which cushion the forceful blow of swords on skulls and coverings for their torsos and eyes to repel the onslaught of small stones launched from hand-held slingshots. Military officers shout injunctions to their troops to ready themselves as the Israelites march slowly towards the city.

Tension and terror mount as some of the people faint and quake with fear, trembling, and vomiting. Pandemonium and chaos ensue behind the walls of Jericho as military spotters announce the advancing sea of Israelites moving deftly towards their city.

As the people march down to the base of the valley, Joshua raises his sheet music in his left hand high over his head, then signals the priests with his right hand to begin their march around the wall seven times. The sun cooks at 110 degrees. The scene is set for the storming of Jericho. Joshua admonishes the people to say nothing until signaled. The priests will sing their songs and play their chords as they march around the city, and the people will resound one long hallelujah, Holy Ghost shout at the top of their lungs after the seventh circumference of the city.

The priests begin their slow march around the city as the Canaanites are baffled, perplexed, even astounded by this unorthodox military maneuver. "What are they doing?" shouts their commander. "I don't know," shouts another." "The fools are walking in circles." "Are they serious?" asks one. "They've got hymn books, prayer books, and scores of sheet music." "Got to be half out of their minds," says another. "Is this some kind of joke?" "We'll blow the whole lot of them to smithereens." "If they think this is some kind of game, they're in for a licking," shouts an infantryman while sharpening his saber.

The priests are marching, circling the city, several carrying the Ark of the Covenant, while those with ram's horn trumpets lead.

Circle one. The joy of the undertaking is fresh upon them. They see the heavenly apocalypse break in victoriously like a Pentecostal epiphany!

Circle two. Their steps get brisker and lighter as they think about how far God has brought them for the battle. They know the march to the fight is longer than the fight. But God has charged their steps like quicksilver on desert oases!

Circle three. The hallelujah choruses of heavenly hosts, with their incantational refrain, hold a board meeting in the sky, while angels claim their clouds over the city as front row seats!

Circle four. This one's for the Gippers: Moses, Abraham, Isaac and Jacob!

Circle five. I've got shoes! You've got shoes! Everybody's got shoes! "We're marching to Zion, beautiful, beautiful Zion. We're marching upwards to Zion, the beautiful city of God!"

Circle six. Not my mama, not my daddy, but it's me, oh Lord, standing in the need of prayer. Not my aunt, not my uncle, but it's me, oh Lord, standing in the need of prayer. My mama couldn't see it. My daddy couldn't see it, but we're gonna see it, Lord!

Circle seven. One big joy song! One loud, long trumpet blast! One long hallelujah shout, and the walls came tumbling down!

What a sight it was! After the seventh circle around the city, the priests blew as hard as they could on their ram's horn trumpets and the people released one long, continuous shout, and the walls fell to the earth in one loud crash. The people in Jericho were shocked and dismayed. As the walls came down, Joshua shouted to the people to charge the city and to spare no one. The siege of

Jericho would be one of the greatest in biblical history. Oddsmakers were stunned. Matchmakers thunderstruck.

No woman, man, or child was spared in the conquest. God was put out with the Canaanites for their idolatrous and rebellious ways. The impossible had been achieved through impossible means. It was a great day for the Israelites, for they had journeyed long and hard to get to this point. They had awaited this moment for forty years, and now God had bestowed the blessing of victory through very unorthodox methods.

What was the real purpose of this conquest? How could God provide such victory against such precarious conditions? What was the underlying meaning of this story? Why did God give Joshua all these complicated and intricate instructions for the storming of Jericho?

First, God chose different leaders for conquest by using the clergy to lead the battle and claim the victory. God wanted it perfectly clear that the people's victory depended on spiritual leadership. Here God allowed the people to claim victory by relying on the priests to lead them.

The clergy led the battle carrying the Ark of the Covenant. The clergy blew the trumpets. The clergy had a primary role in winning the war.

The priests led the battle because God wanted the spirituality of the people to become the primary focus of their conquest. God had anointed the clergy to take an important role in this victory. God's spiritual plan took precedence over the military plan. The military leaders had to rely upon the spiritual leaders for direction and impetus. God wanted it this way, for God knew how inclined the people were to disobey their leadership, as in the case of Moses. God knew that God had to re-establish the authority of the clergy if the people were to enjoy success in the new land, and that's why God had them lead the way in the first conquest in Canaan.

Our march to victory as the people of God depends more upon God and God's appointed and anointed leaders than we care to admit. Yes, we are all, clergy and laity, instruments of God's will and purposes if we are open to God's will. But too quickly, in the give and take of church life, we forget that God has called clergy to lead the people towards spiritual victory and that victory depends upon the willingness of the people to follow and obey their leadership, especially if that leadership is doing the right thing and is consecrated and committed to doing God's will. God had called and consecrated Joshua and the priests to lead God's people to victory. Clergy must lead the way. Clergy must hear the call to battle. The clergy must stand tall amid the seething fires of spiritual warfare and lead the people of God into the promised land of their spirituality.

The clergy leading the way meant that God was still in charge and the people would have to rely completely on the wisdom of God and God's leaders to get them through.

Some of the people may have thought the battle plan foolish — that no victory could ever be claimed under such conditions. But with God anything is possible. What appears as God's foolishness is wiser than man's greatest wisdom. To claim a victory we must have absolute trust in God, and rely on spiritual leadership to get us through. The practice of priests leading the people into battle was very unusual. That's why the Canaanites were baffled by what they saw. They thought the whole thing was a joke. But when the walls came tumbling down, they saw that God was doing a new and miraculous thing among them. It was no joke. God was for real.

If God is leading the way and if we put our absolute trust in God, God can use us in ways which will effect a victory. God can use us for miraculous purposes and bring about a significant change in the lives of those around us. Don't become startled and dismayed if God requires of us something new and different. God's strategies and methodologies will effect positive results.

Some things God gives us the ability to do. Other things require absolute dependence on God and knowing how to tarry, pray, and wait for instructions from God before making a move.

God employed a different strategy for victory for the Israelites, and the effectiveness of such would depend on their trust in God and reliance on the clergy to lead them in battle.

Second, God's miraculous methods were possible because the people had spiritually prepared themselves for battle.

145

The spiritual walk is a battle with ourselves and others for spiritual victory.

The Canaanites were stunned by the battle strategy because nothing in their religious practices or spirituality prepared them for the impossible.

Their religion could not mentally, spiritually, or physically prepare them to accept miracles or to be utilized in miraculous ways. They had neither the headset nor mindset to accept God's working in that way. Nor could they fathom how God could use people in such ways, especially for a fight.

But the Israelites had been spiritually prepared both to be used as instruments of God's miraculous purposes and to be recipients of God's miracles. You will recall in Joshua 3:5, he exhorted them to *consecrate* themselves, for God would do miraculous and amazing things. God also enjoined them to *concentrate* on God's word as a source of strength and preparation. These two things would prepare them to be used by God miraculously and to receive the miracles of God working outside of them.

If you consecrate yourselves for service and concentrate yourselves on God's work, God can use you for miracles.

The Israelites had already done their spiritual homework. They were psychologically and spiritually ready to do the impossible. For they knew through diligent spiritual preparation that a miracle from God was simply a way of raising their expectations of what God could do.

The problem with the Canaanites was that nothing in their religious practices, which were crude and venomous, prepared them to raise their spiritual and faith expectations.

Not the Israelites. Their expectations about God's power of deliverance were already raised. They saw what God did for them in Egypt, in the wilderness, and crossing the Jordan. Their God was a God of great expectations. They knew from experience that God could do the possible amid the impossible. So the possibilities of miracles were not remote. Their spiritual instruction and diligent preparation through prayer, scripture study, fasting, cleansing, and other methods of consecration had put them in the right frame of mind. With God anything was possible, even the toppling of

Jericho's walls on a major or minor chord. For that reason the Canaanites were baffled, but the Israelites were ready.

While the Canaanites were having seizures, the people of God were seizing the city.

As the church moves forward as a community of faith and girds itself for the struggles and battles ahead, you must prepare yourselves spiritually. We cannot succeed for future challenges unless you consecrate and concentrate yourselves on God's will for you.

Nothing is worse than a community which has all the potential for outstanding success but which throttles itself through inadequate spiritual preparation. We have seen time and again the long litany of dismal human failure where individuals who have all the promise and power to do great things sell themselves short or fall shy of their mark because of inadequate preparation. They have low expectations of God and thus have low expectations of themselves, because they have not consecrated themselves spiritually and concentrated themselves in the word of God.

The miracle of Jericho's storming just didn't happen. A long preparation process preceded that victory, and that's something the enemies of God often take for granted. God is a God of preparation.

In order for God to use us the best way God desires, the people of God must spiritually prepare themselves to claim the victory.

Third, God chose different weapons for conquest by using joy songs, trumpets, and hallelujah shouts to bring down the walls of Jericho. Just as God used the clergy to lead the battle, God would use entirely different weapons as instruments to claim the victory. Not swords, not slingshots, not daggers and rocks, but hymn books, trumpet blasts, and hallelujah shouts. Songs, prayers, music, marching and shouting were the weapons.

God used new leaders, new strategies, and new battle plans that discomfited the enemy and gave the Israelites victory. Trusting God means relying on God even if God requires you to do something in a new way. Sometimes we have to change. Sometimes we have to try new things. Sometimes we have to part with tradition in order to meet the requirements God places on us.

147

The great protracted struggle is for the people of God to follow God completely; to place unchanging trust in his power of deliverance. We human beings have been endowed with free will, with a mind of our own. The paradox is it often gets us into deep trouble. Too much free will and too much mind of our own and not enough of God's will veers us off the spiritual path. Sometimes we stay too close to a particular tradition and it stifles growth, progress, and development.

What if the Israelites refused to change and kept their own battle plans? They would have been thoroughly beaten by their enemies. Your enemy can destroy you just in your refusal to look at things a new way. The greatest game of the devil in the church is to pit the traditionalists against the progressives. He's torn many a church apart on this basic premise.

The people of Israel followed the plan to a T. They responded to their leadership. They didn't squawk or balk. They followed through on the plan and vision as given to Joshua and the other leadership anointed to guide them.

If we trust God completely, if we spend a little time talking it over with Jesus, if we put our hand in God's hand and humbly, humbly, humbly ask the Lord to direct our paths, God will show the way.

Where do the people of God go wrong? We don't trust God completely when God wants us to do new things, to employ new strategies to discomfit our enemies. Why are plans blown and why do objectives fail? We don't trust God completely. In our image-conscious society, we dare not appear too foolish or ridiculous for the things of God lest we are ridiculed and rebuked by the larger society. That's why Paul said when all was said and done that he was a fool for Christ's sake. He didn't care what others thought. He knew the Lord. He knew the Lord was able to deliver him in times of trouble. That's why the Israelites didn't mind carrying their hymn books into battle and their trumpets into battle and the people didn't mind giving a Holy Ghost shout. They trusted God so much that they didn't mind looking foolish to their enemies. And look what God did!

The joy songs reminded them of the sweet melodies of God's everlasting graces, the harmony which comes through the unity of

God's people. The trumpets were instruments which allowed them to harmonize the jangling discords of military defeat, and the shout symbolized how the power of their testimony in the heat of battle would bring down the walls that separated them from their greatest dreams. Some joy songs, trumpets, and hallelujah shouts were the only weapons they had, and God gave them the victory.

With Israel God employed new leadership strategy by employing clergy to lead the battle. This was so that the people placed spiritual matters first and relied completely on God. Israel had spiritually prepared themselves through consecration and concentration. With the joy songs, trumpet blasts, and hallelujah shouts, God was using new weapons of war for bringing down the enemy!